Sex Online

Fun with
Adult Friend Finder
and
Other Swinging Sites

Nemo Noone

The Library of Congress has catalogued this book as follows:

Noone, Nemo.
Sex Online: Fun with Adult Friend Finder and Other Swinging Sites.
Nemo Noone — 1st ed.
Includes bibliographical references.
ISBN 1453802622
EAN-13 9781453802625
1. Extramarital Sex. 2. Sex (Psychology). I. Title.

Contents

Introduction

If you can't wait to find out how to have fun on-line with Adult Friend Finder, feel free to skip to chapter one.

There was a time when adolescents had very little access to sex except masturbating or watching the barnyard bulls and rams in action. Later there were collections of "French postcards" purchased during visits to big cities. There were nudist and naturist magazines and perhaps an occasional stag film. Some had access to dirty books. In the early 70s hundreds of cities had X-rated movie theatres. Then came videos in the late 70s, then DVDs. Magazines like *Playboy* have taught two generations of boys to expect their girlfriends and wives to have a polished, airbrushed physical beauty few women actually have, and in so doing they may have inadvertently led to many divorces.

No form of sexual entertainment has had a more potent effect, however, than online pornography. The women of *Playboy* and *Penthouse* were limited in number and highly polished. Novels required people to use a little imagination. For awhile, x-rated films were in theatres, and videos and later DVDs had to be rented and returned or purchased. With the growth of the internet in the mid-90s, though, and especially with an increasing number of people having high-speed access, internet pornography has exploded. It's right there on the desk. It's much harder for adolescents to see now than it was a few years ago, but there are still ways to find it.

Meanwhile, statistics compiled by Jerry Ropelato show that forty million Americans visit internet pornography sites quite often. One survey shows that 53% of the members of Promise Keepers polled admitted that they viewed pornography online at least weekly, and 47% of Christians polled claimed that pornography was a big problem in their homes. It's said that 25% of requests for online searches are for pornography, and 35% of all the downloads from the internet are pornographic. More than 12% of the websites on the internet are pornographic, and they total 372 million pages. Is this just a male problem? Is pornography primarily a crime against women? Almost a third of those visiting pornographic web sites are women—9.4 million women per month—and there are twice as many women in x-rated chat rooms as men (see "Internet Pornography Statistics). For scholarly surveys and analyses, see the work by Al Cooper and his team and of Julie M. Albright in the bibliography.

A Forrester Research Report from 2001 claimed that the average age of those looking at internet pornography was 41, and the average annual income was about $60,000 a year. The National Opinion Research Letter has claimed that in 2002, one in four Americans saw an x-rated film. In a 2003 survey, the Barna Research Group found that 38% of those interviewed see nothing morally wrong with viewing pornography. In a *Christianity Today* survey in 2000, a third of pastors admitted having viewed internet pornography, and 18% viewed it regularly. Patrick Means conducted a confidential survey of conservative evangelical Christian pastors and church leaders. He claims that 64% of them admitted having a problem with pornography. In 2002, Rick Warren's website www.pastors.com did a survey of more than 1,500 pastors. He claimed that 54% of the pastors admitted that they had looked at online pornography that year, and 30% of those during the previous month. That means your pastor may be more like you than you thought.

We need to be cautious about statistics such as these, as they come from anti-pornography sites that are often quite alarmist and take as their starting point that watching pornography is morally wrong. I'm not going to argue that viewpoint here. I give the statistics not to show that there is a problem (though I am concerned about the almost addictive nature of internet pornography viewing, as it can easily interfere with work or family), but to show that there are millions of American adults interested in internet pornography, a third of them women. (For a scholarly analysis of an online *Elle* magazine/MSNBC survey of internet sex usage, see Julie M. Albright. She reports that in a survey of 15,000 people, 75% of the males and 41% of the females had deliberately chosen to look at online erotic photos at least once (p. 181). Of course, some may have never looked again.)

Psychologists Thomas V. Hicks and Harold Leitenberg have done a significant study about sexual fantasies. They used questionnaires completed by 349 people who were in long-term heterosexual relationships (the average length was 9.4 years). About half were married. 215 were female and 134 male. 147 were college students and 202 university employees. The average age of the students was 19. The average age of the employees was about 43. By "fantasy" they meant a brief or elaborate story involving some sort of sexual activity.

They discovered that 98% of men and 80% of women reported having sexual fantasies in the previous two months—different but substantial for both genders. Men reported having about 77 fantasies per month, while women reported having about 34 fantasies. 54% of the men reported having fantasies about people who were not their partners. 36% of the women had that sort of fantasy. Of the non-partner fantasies, women reported that a third of their fantasies were about previous partners, but two thirds were about people who had not been their partners. Note that while men were much more likely than women to fantasize, 80% of these attached women were fantasizing, on average they were having one fantasy a day, and two thirds of these women were fantasizing about men other than their partners. These statistics on fantasies about non-partners fit closely with the statistics about who is viewing internet pornography.

And was there a relationship between fantasizing and acting out the fantasy? Hicks and Leitenberg write, "Contrary to expectations, a nearly identical percentage of men and women (28% vs. 29%) had engaged in extradyadic [outside the couple] sexual behavior or cheated on their current partner." These figures may differ from other estimates because they defined "cheating" as "any type of sexual or romantic encounter with someone other than your current partner ranging from kissing to intercourse." Given that people who kiss non-partners are probably also interested in going farther but restrained by circumstances, this is a more accurate way to gauge interests and willingness than only counting those who have had sexual intercourse.

While Hicks and Leitenberg were primarily interested in gender differences, we should note that while there are gender differences, huge numbers of both men and women are exhibiting this behavior. This is not solely a male interest.

The advice in this book is based on my interviewing hundreds of people in a friendly, informal way, rather than on systematic interviewing and analysis of statistics. It's good advice, and if you follow it, you are much more likely to do very well on Adult Friend Finder and other swinging sites than if you don't. Meanwhile, I have ended my research, and I am no longer involved with the online swinging community. The research was fascinating, though, and I met a lot of wonderful people. Thank you to everyone who helped me. Have fun, folks.

Chapter 1:
Fun with Adult Friend Finder

If you are primarily interested in meeting someone with whom you can share love and romance, perhaps long-term, you need to join a dating site. I recommend www.match.com, where I found my own significant other, but there are several other good ones. On the other hand, if you want to meet someone for sex, you need to read this book. By the time you've finished it, you'll be able to avoid the mistakes so many people make and actually meet people and have fun. If you don't, good luck. Chances are you'll be disappointed.

Internet pornography is easy to find, so there's no need for this book to offer directions. What's more, because merely viewing it is a solitary act, it's not of major interest to us. In this chapter I want to focus on internet sites offering personal ads from swingers. A useful list of web sites dealing with swinging and polysexuality in a variety of forms can be found at http://www.nasca.com/states/nasca_internet.html (NASCA International is an umbrella organization of swingers. Its logo has an apple with a bite out of it [recalling Adam and Eve in the garden of Eden] and the amusing slogan, "For those who want more than just one bite.")

Rather than survey a bunch of these sites (they have many similarities), I will concentrate on one. AdultFriendFinder (AFF) is huge and worldwide. (By contrast, another popular option, SwingLifeStyle [SLS] is much smaller, and the photos and descriptions are tamer, but it is aimed more specifically—though not exclusively—at swinging couples. It seems to have a higher proportion of "real" members [members who are not escorts or promoting their web sites and who actually do meet with people, rather than just teasing people or fantasizing].)

AdultFriendFinder bills itself as "The World's Largest Sex & Swinger Personals Site." It is surprisingly worldwide. On 6 February 2006, for example, it claimed 5,437 listings for Albania, 782 listings for Burundi, 139,070 listings for Egypt, 1,012 listings for Azerbaijan, 87,500 listings for China (of which 52,596 were men seeking women and 3,210 were women seeking men), 47,732 listings for Israel, 15,992 listings for Iraq, 15,226 listings for Saudi Arabia, and 5,818 listings for Afghanistan.

The company that operates AFF (it was recently purchased by Penthouse) also operates FriendFinder (4 million members interested in dating and romance—no nude photos allowed) and ALT.com (3.6 million members interested in bondage, discipline, sadism, masochism, and/or a huge number of other fetishes). It operates OutPersonals (adult gay personal ads) and Gay Friendfinder (PG rated gay personals). It also operates Amigos.com (Spanish and Portuguese friendship and dating ads), Asia FriendFinder, Indian Friend-Finder, Korean, German, French, Filipino, and Italian versions. It even operates Senior FriendFinder, Jewish FriendFinder, and BigChurch.com ("Bringing people together in love and faith"—the questionnaire offers, as options, meeting a man or woman for "a dating relationship, marriage, a friend, a bible study partner, pen pals, a prayer partner"). The numbers given for AFF also seem to include Passion.com (as they have the same numbers, though not the same memberships), and this may skew some of the percentages given below.

On 6 February 2006, AdultFriendFinder claimed about 21 million members around the world and 13 million in the United States (about 34 million and 16 million respectively in August 2010—the numbers are rising quickly, but the percentages below should stay close to constant). On 6 February 2006, in the U.S., there were 6,454,000 men seeking women for sex (50% of the total membership). There were 404,000 men seeking men (3.1%, but note that many of these are also seeking women and couples). There were 915,000 men seeking couples (7%).

By contrast, there were only 552,000 women seeking men (4.2% of the total 13 million). There were 428,000 women seeking other women (3.3%, though most of those were also seeking men) and 153,000 women seeking couples (1.2%).

There were 120,000 couples seeking men (0.9%). Some 557,000 couples were seeking women (4.3%). There were 394,000 couples seeking other couples (3%). (The numbers for these don't add up, as there are many other options. For example, many people are not seeking people for sex, but for erotic chat, e-mail, and phone calls.)

The ratio of men seeking women to women seeking men is 11.7:1. The ratio of men seeking couples to couples seeking men is 7.6:1. The ratio of couples seeking women to women seeking couples is 3.6:1.

On AFF, all members (or couples) have their own web page. At the top of the page is their handle, age, and place of residence. There is also a summary of the sort of people they are looking for (for example, to quote one, "Looking For: Women, Couples (man and woman) or Groups for 1-on-1 sex, Group sex (3 or more!) or Exhibition/Voyeurism"). This sort of categorization allows for detailed searches. On their page they can have multiple photos, as tame or wild as they like. They can also now post videos of themselves. They write a profile of themselves (or get help from AFF, which leads to repetition) and also write out what they are looking for. They can add more information about their favorite sexual fantasies, their favorite toys, the bedroom activities that most interest them or repel them, what factors most interest them in a partner, and many more.

The personal ad page also includes information on sexual orientation, marital status, height, body type, smoking, drinking, education, occupation, race, religion, children, male endowment, and language preferred. (Oddly, one can search for possible partners according to breast or penis size, height, weight, ethnicity, and many other possibilities, but not by education, type of work, income, or social class. The assumption seems to be that when it comes to sex, these things don't matter.) The astrological sign is given (astrology buffs must hope the birth date given is correct). More useful, perhaps, is the questionnaire used to establish personality type, based on the Meyers-Briggs Type

Indicator (MBTI). Having taken the complete MBTI, administered by a professional, I took the AFF version to see if it assigned the same personality type. It did, even though my type makes up only about 1% of the population.

There are three levels of membership in AFF: standard, silver, and gold. Standard is free. At present, silver is $100 for a year and gold $150. You get what you pay for.

Many people join AFF thinking they will be able to see millions of ads and send messages to everyone they please. Not true. The ads of standard members look about the same as the others. What differs is what they can see of other people's ads. Standard members can search within a wide range of parameters, such as distance, ethnic origin, language, and age. They receive the same search results: a list of people with a tiny photo, their handle and one sentence description, age, where they live, and what they are looking for.

However, standard members don't get to see people's entire pages, full profiles, large photos, or anything. What's more, standard members cannot initiate messages. They can respond to messages (ten per day), but they do so without seeing the information listed above. If standard members see someone they like, they can send a "wink." A wink may mean "I like your looks" or "I'd like to meet you" or "Write me and let's see if we are compatible." But most winks are never responded to, and many people never send winks (though some people seem to wink at nearly every person whose ad they view).

A great many men are standard members, and even more women. Although it's a bad decision, a woman can get away with being a standard member, as gold and silver members can see her ad and write to her. She can't see their ads, though, so deciding whether people are worth meeting is more difficult. She can initiate contact with gold and silver members by sending a wink, but while she can send a wink to a standard member, that member can't respond. What's the sense of winking at someone who can't respond?

Here are some statistics based on samples from around the U.S. Only 3% of women with AFF ads are gold or silver members, but 75% of those are active. Women who pay are serious about meeting people, so they stay active. (I am defining active as having been on AFF within the past week. Many people check their ads several times a day. Those who don't check their ads at least weekly have lost interest or given up. As they are unlikely to answer a message, they should not be considered active.) Of the 97% of women who are standard members, only 18% are active. The total percentage of active women is 19.7%. That means that about 80% of the women supposedly "on AFF" are no longer seeking.

They are no longer part of the dating pool. While only 1.2% of the total women are seeking couples, 3.2% of the active women are seeking couples.

The comparisons between women and men are instructive. While 7.8% of men are gold or silver members, compared to 3% of the women, the ratio between men and women who are gold or silver members is 31:1. Many more men are paid members. Of the men who are gold or silver members, 62% are active (compared to 75% of the women). This difference may be because men are more likely to buy a membership, then leave in disappointment when they don't get many (or any) responses. By contrast, women who are gold or silver members are sure to get responses, so they are more likely to remain active. Of the men who are standard members, only 6.7% are active (compared to 18% of the women who are standard members). This is probably because standard members can see virtually nothing and can't initiate messages. As very few women who are gold or silver members write to men who are standard members, most of these men get no messages and leave disappointed. The total percentage of men who are active is 11%.

While the ratio of all men seeking women to all women seeking men is 11.7:1, the ratio of men who are active gold or silver members seeking women to women who are active gold, silver, or standard members seeking men is only 3:1. This is the ratio that matters. There is one active woman for every three paying and active men. Among men, only active paid members count. This is because only men or couples who can contact people really count, given how rare it is for women to contact men or couples. The rest of the men are losers, drones. The men who pay can disregard them, as they provide no threat, no competition. If you are a man, you simply will not succeed on AFF unless you buy a membership.

A full 21.7% of couples are gold or silver members, and 81% of these are active, while only 23.5% of the couples who are standard members are active. In total, 28% of couples who are ostensibly AFF members are active. (Couples seeking men or couples can get away with being standard members because men and couples who are gold or silver members can contact them—and do. Couples who are standard members seeking women are unlikely to find what they're looking for.) The ratio of couples who are active gold or silver members seeking women to active women who are seeking couples is 2.7/1. The ratio of active men who are gold or silver members seeking couples to active couples seeking men is 10/1. This means it is more than three times harder for a man to find a couple than for a man to find a woman. Only 9.6% of the active couples are seeking a man.

Who is looking? An attractive forty year old man in decent condition with a well-written ad and good photos who is a silver or gold member will be fortunate if 250 people look at his ad in the course of a year. Of that 250, half may be other men who enjoy looking (even if the man isn't interested in other men). Of that 250, perhaps eight "real" people will send a wink (five of them men). (There are many young women whose job is to wink at people on AFF and try to get them to join some web site. These women are not "real.") If the man sends a message to the three "real" women who wink, one might reply. This man may not receive a single unsolicited message from a woman in the entire year.

It's common for a man to join AFF as a standard member filled with fantasies of getting dozens of messages from eager women. Perhaps he wants to be discreet, so he has no photo on his ad, and his profile is brief and stresses how horny he is. For the first week he visits the site ten times a day. Then he realizes no one is looking, he realizes that he can't see other people's ads, and he discovers that he can't write to other people, so he gives up.

Or perhaps he is determined to be successful. He pays for a gold or silver membership. He looks at what other people have written, then rewrites his ad. He puts some decent (or indecent) photos of himself on the ad, he takes some of the tests available and posts the results. Now he thinks hundreds will look at him and dozens will write. Instead, three guys wink at him in the first month and no one writes.

So this man convinces his girlfriend to put together a couples ad, just to see what will happen. He knows how to write a good ad now, and he puts some interesting photos of her on the ad. What happens? The first day, their ad gets seventy messages. This gradually decreases until after a couple weeks, they are only getting about ten or fifteen a day. However, people from around the world are looking, and at the end of a year they discover that 15,000 people have viewed their ad.

Women get much the same result, but greater. However, a woman should figure that if she doesn't have a photo on her ad, she will only get a tenth as many responses, and the ones she does get may be from the most hard-up men, not the ones she most wants to meet. The majority of men on AFF have things set up so they only see people with photos. Why look at people without photos? Writing a message, getting acquainted, then asking for a photo is too much work, given that so few women reply. There are solid reasons why men and women don't want their photos on their ads, but they need to be aware that without photos, very few people will write to them. Women and couples who are gold or silver members also get more messages, primarily because their ads show up earlier in a search. A woman who is a standard member but has photos will get more responses than a woman who is a gold member but has no photos, but she will do best if she is a gold or silver member and also has photos. Not only are gold and silver members more likely to be seen, but they are more likely to be "real."

Some AFF members claim that for security reasons, a woman is crazy to not invest in a paid membership. Members can have part of their profiles attached to messages they send, but there is a lot of information on some ads that doesn't show up in messages and that a prospective date might do well to study. For example, if you aren't a paid member, you could end up agreeing to meet with a man without realizing that he is a heavy drinker and smoker who is married with young children and fond of urolagnia. He insists on wearing high heels, nylons, garter belt, and a bra while having sex, and he has a three inch erection and a pierced penis with a large ring in it. This is fine if this is what interests you, but if you wait until your date before discovering this, your date is likely to be disappointing. Even the most apparently perfect people are often less than ideal. Why make the odds even higher?

As for men, paid members often put it this way. "How much does it cost you to take a woman to a nice restaurant for dinner, with wine, bring her flowers, take her dancing, buy her a few drinks?

Over $100? Over $200? And that's for one night, and you still don't know if you'll have sex with her. Or what does it cost to take her to a movie, then out for pizza and beer? Maybe $50? And again, maybe she won't even give you a kiss at the end of the evening. Or what does it cost to go to a dance club, pay the cover, buy drinks for yourself, buy drinks for several women? It can be expensive, and you still may go home alone. What's more, if you are forty or fifty, will you be welcome in the club? Will there be any women your age or who are interested in men your age?"

If a man wants to meet new partners, the $100 it costs for a year's membership on AFF or a similar site is cheap, given the possible results. There is also the pleasure to be had, even if one never meets anyone else, from looking at people's full ads. Women and couples, of course, also enjoy this pleasure. I can't stress this enough: Men, don't even bother with AFF or similar sites unless you buy a membership. If you are too much of a cheapskate to do that, just stay home with your hand. You're a loser. And women, isn't your safety and fun worth $100 for a year?

There are other things to do on AFF besides try to get dates. There are, for example, chat rooms, categorized by location and topic of interest. For example, at this moment, as I write, there are 86 people in the Texas chat room and 18 people in the Alaska chat room. Only one lonely person is in the Finland chat room. There are 128 men (only men) in the Bath House chat room, 14 people in the Basement, for B&D fans, 15 in the clean room (no sex talk allowed), 16 in the Love Doctors room, where people can get health advice (from each other). There are 22 in the Mature room (over 50), and 7 in the Brawl Room (Is this the right room for an argument?).

There is also a Group page with thousands of links. Some of these are chat rooms, and some of them are for leaving messages that can be read and enjoyed (or not) for months. At this moment there are 171 people chatting about "Girls Watching Guys Cum on Cam" and 7 chatting about "Peeing Pleasures" in the "Watersports" interest group. There are 38,238 groups listed in the U.S., divided by state, region, and sometimes county or city. Some of these are very active; others haven't had a post in months. This is a good way to find out where the parties are. It's sometimes possible to arrange a meeting online and meet the person an hour later. There are adult directories for every region, and members can review the establishments. Groups are a good way to have a discussion about your particular interests. Many people find that their needs are adequately met by talking about them, whether or not there is any sexual excitement or release.

Another popular part of AFF is the online Magazine. Members contribute thousands of comments about such topics as Breaking Up, Building a Relationship, First Date, and Safe Sex. They can contribute jokes, poems, rants, and erotic stories. The most popular posters receive the honor of having a link to their ad posted with their photo on the magazine page. There are also professionally written articles about various aspects of sexuality.

Many AFF members who have given up on meeting people are active posters on the advice boards. Some of them are intelligent and thoughtful. Unfortunately, their posts are less popular than they deserve. It seems amazing at times that with 34 million members, so few people have anything to say. (Actually, probably most of them have better things to do with their lives.) There are also the posters who ask such penetrating questions as "Do you like to have orgasms?" or "What's your favorite position?" Some of the brighter posters occasionally rant at them or wither them with sarcastic comments—it's hard to resist. Despite the difficulties, the Magazine sometimes provides useful answers to such burning questions as "What's the best lubrication for anal sex?"

A recent addition to AFF is the ability to create blogs. Any member can develop a blog or comment on one. However, men soon discover that virtually no one reads their blogs. All of the top fifteen blogs are written by women or couples. It's interesting to note the age of the writers, though. There are two in their 20s, six in their 30s, four in their 40s, two in their 50s (including the most popular blog), and one who claims to be 94 (but isn't).

The Hotlist allows people to quickly and easily mark people they'd like to consider when they have more leisure or to mark profiles or photos they enjoy and want to save. If people add you to their hotlist, then when you click on "Who's Been Looking at Me," a link to their ad will show up. This is a great way to discover that someone is interested. If the person is a standard member, one can take the initiative and send a message. Unfortunately, lately there are young women who are not "real" who are adding thousands of people a day to their Hotlists. Then these "professionals" from California or Thailand have their photos on your list of those who have Hotlisted you, and you can't get rid of them.

Another nice feature of AFF is the Network, or list of Friends. Whenever you send a message, you have the option of inviting the person to join your network and become one of your friends. This can be a good way to not lose track of people you want as long-term acquaintances. In many cases, the

Network doesn't matter, but sometimes it's very useful. AFF members are allowed to post photo albums that can be seen only by people in their networks. Standard members can post five photos in an album, silver members twenty, and gold members fifty. By clicking on Friends, one can quickly see which friends have posted new photos of themselves. One can also find out who has good albums and ask them to be in one's network.

Another useful aspect of your network is that unless those in your network have turned off access to those in their networks, you can see the ads of all their friends. Does this matter? Well, perhaps they have some peculiar tastes, and you want to meet other people with tastes like that. Or say you are a woman who wants a partner who is a straight male. A man who writes to you says he is straight, but you look on his network and see that most of the people there are not straight. This might lead you to be cautious.

One popular feature on AFF is the webcams. Members can hook up webcams and let themselves be seen. Better yet, they can hook up with other members for a mutual show. (You do not have to be hooked up to a webcam to see other people.) Many members merely have their webcams trained on their faces while they read their messages, smiling or frowning occasionally. Very few people watch these. However, hundreds of people masturbate online at AFF, and a few have male/female sex on line. Some people find this quite satisfying. Often the lighting is poor or the quality of the camera is poor, but sometimes both are quite good. (Caution: if you are using a webcam and want people to enjoy you, turn on all the lights in the room and shine a few on the main point of interest. You can't easily have too much light, but most people have too little. This makes the video grainy and unclear.)

It's interesting to note who is using webcams. At this moment, of the 34 million AFF members, there are 1,612 members from around the world using webcams. There are 1,407 men, 41 women, 149 couples (male/female), 2 male/male couples, 1 group, and 10 transvestites. Women can often draw 200 viewers just by flirting a little. Men are lucky to draw one viewer, whatever they do.

Those who are on cam can see who is watching and how they are being rated. People on cam can also block people who are watching. It's rather amusing that on occasion men get very angry that other men are watching them masturbate. They rant about this now and then in the advice columns. The thing is, it's rare for a woman to show up to watch a man masturbate, so if a man is waiting around on his webcam for a woman, he's not going to be ready when she shows up.

Most of the men masturbating on webcams claim to be straight, yet they know they will probably be seen only by other men. This any-port-in-a-storm philosophy—better to be watched by a man than by no one—is similar to the one that leads otherwise straight men frustrated by the lack of response to their ads to meet occasionally with another man for mutual pleasure. While this may seem appalling to many men, there are a great many more men who are to a greater or lesser degree bi-sexual than there are men who are gay. Just as they often don't connect extramarital sex with any loss of interest in or affection for their spouse, so they often don't see this as homosexual behavior. Indeed, many of these men would not meet with an avowedly homosexual man, preferring other married men.

Is there any advice worth sharing with men who are interested in joining AFF and want to actually meet people? Yes, a lot. This is gleaned from conversations with members and from following the advice columns. You do need to join, and you'd be crazy to not buy a silver or gold membership. A gold membership will get you higher positioning in searches, but given that very few women are gold or silver members able to see your ad, that isn't very important.

Good photos are important, but the definition of good varies. Many women appreciate a photo of a man's face on an ad—indeed, a pleasant face in a well-taken photo will draw more women than a hot body without a face—but many men are not comfortable putting their face on their ad page. If they don't, they will draw less interest. Many women appreciate a nude rear view of a man, but some people consider that a covert signal that the man is interested in men as well as women. A full-body frontal or side nude is appreciated, as it lets women see your shape. There is a big argument over "cock shots." Many women claim to despise them, but a much larger percentage loves them. What the women seem to agree on, though, is that they don't like seeing limp ones. "If that's the best he can do," one woman said, "I'm not biting."

Good poses and lighting are also important. Some poses will emphasize a man's potbelly, thinning hair, or double chin, while other poses are more attractive. Many men shave their genitals, and in the wrong light the result can look a lot like a naked turkey ready for the oven on Thanksgiving Day or an uncooked sausage—not very appetizing. If you want to look classy, make sure the surrounding area is neat and clean. Suck in your gut. Try to look warm, friendly, and huggable. Wear a dress shirt and pants and just reveal a little of yourself. It's important to have more than one photo, but less important than for women. Remember that because most women are standard members, they will only see a photo of you about an inch tall. Make sure the good things about yourself can be seen in a photo that small. If not, crop the photo or use a different one.

Fill out everything you can about yourself, as this can help women get a sense of who you are. Most important is your profile, as you can attach that to any message you may send. Even standard members can read your profile if you attach it to a message. Some men write very brief profiles emphasizing their sexual prowess, such as "I can go for hours." Some claim to be searching for "A nymphomaniac with a gorgeous face and body." Men who work hard to meet women love ads like that because they know these men aren't going to provide competition—few women will bother to respond to them, much less meet them. The exception is perhaps an extremely handsome guy with a terrific body.

There are plenty of women on AFF who are eager for sex, but most women want a man who seems like a nice person who doesn't see them as a collection of body parts. Thus, write about how you like to curl up on the couch with your date and watch a "chick flick" (assuming you do). Write about how pleasant and good-natured you are. Tell people you aren't just in this for sex, but above all for friendship. Tell them that while a one-night-stand might be okay on occasion, you really prefer a longer relationship so you can get to know a woman and become special friends. Mention romantic things you like to do: long drives on mountain roads, walks along the beach in the moonlight, wine and candles.

There are guides to help people write AFF profiles, but if you use one, avoid using that exact language. It's become too familiar. When readers come across these profiles, they think, "Oh, another barely literate idiot with no creativity. What a loser." Write your own profile. Make yourself seem likeable, attractive, and good at what you propose to do, but don't boast. Lots of women avoid self-centered men. Be yourself, but be yourself at your best. If you are intelligent, witty, educated, well-read, and into opera, ballet, and international travel, by all means say so (without boasting—hints will do, and they will catch the eye of the few women on AFF who like that sort of thing). But if you aren't, don't lie. People like that intimidate many AFF members.

The majority of women seem to be most interested in men from their own social class and with somewhere near their own level of education. Women with tattoos want men with tattoos. Women who like motorcycles want men who own them. Women who find television entertaining aren't looking for men who would rather read a book. But women want the men they choose to be interesting, thoughtful, fun, and focused on pleasing a woman rather than on "getting laid." They want the man their previous (or present) husband turned out not to be. And remember, while on AFF it's most often the men who first write to the women (because the women aren't generally paid members), AFF is definitely a buyer's market, and you need to do everything you can to make yourself attractive to women. On AFF, it's the women who have the ultimate power of acceptance and rejection. They are really in charge. They are the ones who choose.

When you first look at the AFF web site, you will see several stunning young women, and you will expect to see more after you join and pay. Don't hold your breath. AFF automatically sets up your home page so you see, in the middle, the words "Recent member photo gallery." Unless you change the settings, every morning you will have available the handles, ages, and photos of all the women and couples in your state who have joined AFF and put up photos in the past 24 hours. You may be pleased to find that lots of these eager women are real beauties in their twenties. If you read their profiles, you may decide that they are looking specifically for you.

The problem is that they aren't "real." These beautiful young women are "escorts," phone sex girls, "models," or perhaps they have a web site of their own and will let you see more photos of them or perhaps even watch them masturbate online if you will pay a certain amount per month by credit card with automatic recharging every month. This is just a way of leading you away from AFF and back to the world of internet porn.

I estimate that in my area, 75 percent of the recent members every day are not "real." A few years ago there was a spate of women from Russia and the Ukraine running ads with American addresses. For a year or more most new members were "real." Now they are local "professionals." It used to be just the young ones who weren't "real." Now there are also ads from women in their 30s and 40s who are "professionals," drawing on specialized markets of "older women lovers."

How can you spot the fakes, the women who are in it for the money? Those who have been on AFF for a while agree that it isn't too hard. If the woman is very slim and firm with a beautiful face, if there is only one photo, if that photo looks professionally done with several lights, such as you might see in a porn magazine, if the profile is very short and very hot, if none of the extra features or questionnaires have been filled out, and if the woman is a standard member, the woman is almost certainly a "professional." Indeed, she may have a hundred ads with the same photo but from different towns and states. Don't waste your time (or your money). Look but don't touch. (AFF members usually alert the webmaster about these women within a day or two, and in a few more days their ad is removed, but meanwhile they manage to make money off a few guys who are thinking with their lower brains.)

The handle a woman chooses is a tip-off. "BangMyBoobs" is probably not "real." Neither is "LipsOfXstasy," "BustySex," "SxyNRdy2Lrn," "eZsex," "SteemyNites," "JuciSex," "XoticTreat," "MACyberSlut," "Cum2Hevn," "FillMyKitty," or "IdoWhatUwant." (I've changed these slightly from actual AFF handles, but you get the idea.)

Here are some sample ads from women who are unlikely to be "real." (I've rewritten them, but there are thousands like them, nearly all standard members.)

"I just got out of a horrible relationship. My boyfriend just couldn't satisfy me. I'm looking for a man who not only has a big cock, but has lots of experience and can teach me some bedroom tricks. I want a man who will love me and leave me and be discreet about it. I'm looking for a no-strings relationship." This woman will get hundreds of offers from men who think they can satisfy her. She will invite many of these men to write directly to her e-mail address. Then she will offer to talk with the men online on her own website or offer them photos for money or even offer to meet "generous" men. Meanwhile, she may sell the e-mail addresses of anyone who writes to her, and those men will then receive several thousand spam messages over the course of the next several months.

"My marriage is just terrible. My husband isn't interested in me, and I only have sex with myself. I think I'm attractive, but I can't remember the last time someone told me so. I want a man who can satisfy my fantasies. I can't remember the last time I had an orgasm. I want to try anal. Does it hurt?" This woman is not actually thirty miles away, but probably living in Russia (one tip-off is wallpaper, which is very common in Russia and the Ukraine). Her ad has many characteristic errors that suggest this. "Professional" women in their thirties often use this approach, as it appeals to many men. Foreign women sometimes use it to try to get men to send them money so they can come to America for a "visit."

"I'm a great communicator, but I need someone to talk to. I want to try all the things I've always wanted to try." This is a woman who claims to want erotic chat or e-mail. She probably also wants to be paid for it.

"I just escaped from a bad relationship. I'm sexy, hot, and horny, but the last thing I need right now is another relationship. I don't like going to bars, so I thought I'd try here. If you are in the same situation and are good in bed, maybe we could get together. I'll try anything sexy that isn't too weird." This woman is also probably a "professional," possibly an "escort." Don't be tempted by women like this unless you aren't looking for a "real" woman.

(This might be a good place, guys, for a reality check. Feel free to look at all the photos of sweet young women on AFF, but unless you are near their age, don't bother to write—you'd be wasting your time. You may not realize this, but it's true: to most women of twenty, a man who is twenty-three is "older," and a man of twenty-seven is often so old he is scary. You remind them of their father or grandfather, and they don't want to date their father or grandfather. There are of course young women who like "older men," but very few women in their twenties want to go out with a guy in his forties, and very few women in their thirties want to go out with a guy in his fifties. Feel free to dream, but if you want to score, you need to aim at women within about five years of your age—and don't neglect those who are older. If you are wealthy and looking for some hot young thing to share your yacht or your next trip to Switzerland or Hong Kong, and you are fit and handsome for your age, fine, feel free to write. Money and power can be very attractive. Otherwise, learn to love women your own age—or older.)

By contrast, if the woman is a gold or silver member, if she has more than one photo, if those photos don't look too professional, if she doesn't look like a magazine model, if she has filled out the questionnaires, if she has written an interesting profile that isn't merely about her love of sex, she's probably not a professional. Also, a gold or silver member with multiple photos is more likely to actually meet people.

(A lot of AFF members have good intentions and many offers, but never actually meet with anyone. They may answer messages and contribute to the advice columns and pretend that they are eager to meet, but then they pull back. This seems to be a huge percentage of members, both male and female. They may be shy or unwilling to risk the possible complications of meeting people, though they still enjoy being found attractive.)

In a study of over 15,000 people who filled out online questionnaires on MSNBC, Julie M. Albright found that of those who said they had been on sites like AFF, 30% of the men and 23% of the women failed to meet in person with anyone, though in many cases this may have been their own choice. However, 37% of the men and 36% of the women met one person. Perhaps this was enough to satisfy their curiosity, or perhaps the meeting was unsatisfactory, or perhaps they discovered that this was not what they really wanted. Another 22% of the men and 26% of the women met between two and four people. Finally, 14% of the men and 16% of the women met five or more partners (p. 179). It isn't clear how many of them actually had sex or how many times the respondents met with the same person.)

Phony ads are not limited to women seeking men. A small percentage of ads are aimed at women seeking women. These women are just as "professional," and indeed they may also have a website catering to men. There are some couples who are "professional," as well. They are generally young, very fit, and very attractive. There are quite a few handsome, muscular, and well-endowed young male "professionals" hoping to attract "generous" men, and there are also some transsexuals with similar hopes.

One might expect that with so many men already on AFF, there would be no market for "professional" men hoping to drum up business from "generous" women, but there are some. Unlike with women, a number of these are gold or silver members. (Men will search for hours through the standard ads, but given that there may be hundreds of gold or silver male members within twenty miles of a woman's location, women may never reach standard ads. Thus, a "professional" man needs to invest in a membership in order to be noticed.

Here's a sample ad from a boyish "professional in the entertainment industry" with impressive muscles and enormous genitals. Because women who can afford to pay are likely to be powerful, intelligent, well-traveled, and well-read, the man claims to be seeking that sort of woman. Then he adds, "Age doesn't matter to me. Almost any attractive woman who is looking for mutually rewarding sex interests me. I love women who like to be in control of the situation." (By contrast, a non-professional the same age told me, "I would probably not have a partner more than two years older or ten years younger than myself, but I am both younger and a bit old fashioned." This attitude is understandable and common. However, it leaves a lot of more mature women available for those who enjoy them.)

In addition to the sexual benefits men may get from AFF and similar sites, there are sociological and psychological benefits. One respondent told me, echoing what many have said, "I looked at girls in magazines for years. When I was a teenager, I thought women were supposed to look like the girls in *Playboy*. Of course when I got married, I was disappointed. I kept on looking at pornography after marriage, and most of those girls were between eighteen and twenty-five. I loved sleek, well-toned bodies and firm little breasts. That's pretty much the way I thought women looked with their clothes off—except for my wife, who was the only actual woman I was seeing without clothes.

"My wife was getting into her mid-forties, and when I looked at her I saw the remnants of her former beauty. I saw how her beauty was slipping away. She didn't look much like the girls in the photos. I wondered if I'd even be able to get it up for her in another five years. I guess I was scared by the coming of age. I wasn't ready to have sex with a grandmother. (It never occurred to me to wonder how my wife felt about having sex with a grandfather.)

"When I joined AFF, I first noticed all these great looking girls in their twenties who looked like the magazine girls, and I started writing to them. It never occurred to me to wonder what they would want with a guy who is no fashion model himself and was old enough to be their dad. Many of these girls replied, but they wanted me to pay to talk to them on the phone or to look at photos on their web sites. That's not what AFF promised, and that's not why I joined.

"Then I sort of held my breath and pinched my nose and started looking at the other women. It was quite a shock. What I discovered was that apart from those girls who aren't 'real,' hardly any of the women looked like magazine girls. That's just not the way most adult women look. I was astonished by the rolls of fat around their bellies, their big, floppy breasts, the way that even women in their early twenties sagged. It hadn't really occurred to me that the magazine girls I'd been looking at for years were not average girls, physically, but the shapeliest. The others didn't get chosen by the photographers and editors.

"Gradually, as I looked at thousands of photographs of very real women the way they really look, I began to find them sexy in their own right, for what they are. Then I began to find their bulges and sags actually beautiful in many cases. I began to appreciate big women. Meanwhile, I still appreciate the looks of the firm young girls, but I rarely bother to look at them anymore—just when I feel like tasting a bit of eye candy for a minute. I hardly ever look at pornography anymore—it just seems boring compared to the real thing. What's more, I've come to realize that while my wife may not be as young as she once was, she's still more beautiful than about 99% of the women her age on AFF and in better shape than most of the 'real' women in their twenties."

This seems to be a common experience. Many men have told me something similar. One hears this as well from men who become nudists or naturists. When they start spending time around nudists, they soon stop being aroused by naked skin in non-sexual situations. They break the association between nudity and sex. They also soon gain a much more accurate understanding of what nude people actually look like and what time, lunch, and gravity do to people. Julie M. Albright reports that in her survey of 15,000 people, about a quarter of both the men and the women claimed that looking at erotic images online had improved sex with their partners, and about the same percentage said that looking had made it easier to talk about sex with their partners (p. 181).

Perhaps the most pernicious effect of *Playboy*, *Penthouse*, and pornography has been to firmly implant in men's minds an ideal of beauty that very few women can match. (Even the women in the photos often can't match the ideal, given that the photographs are generally "improved" in some way, whether by lighting, make-up, air-brushing, or computer wizardry. At the least, often hundreds of less-attractive shots are taken for every one that gets printed.)

It must be daunting for women to look at such photos and realize that they are being compared to the best photos of the sexiest girls and found wanting. How many men have decided to leave their wives or girlfriends because they don't meet that ideal? How many men look at their wives when their wives are bathing and consider their bodies far below average—merely because their idea of average is skewed by their viewing habits? This is very sad.

Men really do find that looking at women on AFF gives them a much more accurate idea of what women actually look like and how time affects them. As men come to see women in a new way, they also start being excited by things that did not excite them before. Some men who used to be excited by a protuberant iliac crest on a woman's hip now find themselves more turned on by a roll of fat on a belly. Men who preferred hard round breasts find they can also enjoy flaccid breasts. Men who begin by looking at women in their twenties on AFF find themselves looking with admiration at women in their fifties and sixties. This is a very healthy result, and it would be good for society if all men could develop such realistic views.

The man quoted above went on to tell me, "I used to worry about not finding my wife attractive as she aged. Now I've seen enough older women—and felt attracted to them—that I no longer worry about that. I'm confident that I will always find her lovely and desirable."

One psychological benefit for men who are gold or silver members of AFF is that they can gain an increased sense of self-esteem. As they discover that women find them attractive the way they are and find them sexually satisfying, they gain confidence, and as they gain confidence, they have more success in finding partners. (This is assuming, of course, that they manage to find any partners at all—many don't. This can be hard on their self-esteem.)

Many men have never had much self-esteem. Many have very little sexual experience apart from their wives. Even those who long for sex, if shy or repressed, may be virgins when married, and they may have wives who discourage talking about sex and never give them physical compliments. As they age, lose hair, add pounds, their self-esteem may decrease. They may notice that young women don't even glance at them while passing, much less smile. They may assume that what little virility they had is fading.

Even if there is no meeting, no sex, a man's sense of worth can be increased quite a bit if a woman he doesn't even know offers a few complimentary sentences. One man told me, "I look older than I am, and I'm older than most people on AFF. In my first year, as a standard member, only seven people even looked at my ad. Finally, though, I discovered the advice groups in the Magazine section. I had quite a few partners before I got married, and my wife and I are pretty creative. I started responding to the questions in the advice area in a thoughtful and interesting way, and within a few months I had several hundred posts and was actually rated among the top hundred or so respondents. People started referring to things I'd written, recognizing me, sending me an occasional private message to thank me for writing well. That made me feel pretty good about myself. Of course, these people lived across the country or in different countries, but so what? And people started looking at my ad just to see who had written in the advice pages. I started feeling like I belonged, like I had something to contribute.

"Then I started getting an occasional response from local women, and eventually I met with a few, and a good time was had by all. One woman said she found me really warm and comfortable. Another said that when she saw my photo she almost deleted my message, but she's glad she didn't, because she thought I was a really good lover. I'll tell you—I felt great. And my wife got to enjoy how great I felt that night. It's weird, but while she enjoys sex, I can't remember her ever telling me I was good at it or satisfying."

Another interesting psychological benefit also turns out to be a social benefit. Many men have learned (sometimes the hard way) that many women resent sexist comments, off-color jokes or remarks or innuendoes, or men making passes at work. No woman should have to experience this if she doesn't want to, and very few women wear t-shirts saying "Tell me a dirty joke," so intelligent men know the wisest policy is to never say anything to a woman at work about her appearance unless they are certain it won't be taken wrong. They also know that dating people from work is not a good idea. (If you wonder why, watch the DVD of the movie *Bridget Jones' Diary*.)

Looking and admiring as one walks down the street or shops or works is fine, but it must be done covertly, without giving offense. Wolf whistles and shouted comments are only acceptable in strip clubs. If a man makes a pass at a woman somewhere, he may risk a reprimand from his boss or a sexual harassment grievance. (This is a serious thing for a man, as it can cause great damage to his career. It's also a serious thing for a woman. Women have the right to do their work without sexual harassment or exclusion. Treating women as colleagues rather than as potential sexual partners is the right way to work.)

However, AFF is clearly and officially a sex and swingers site. Some women may be offended by what some men write to them, but they are not likely to be offended because men compliment them or tell them their fantasies. Many men find it liberating to be able to share their feelings with women. They may also find, though, that because they now have an outlet for their sexual feelings, they have no need for an outlet at work. Thus, men who are members of AFF may find that they no longer look at their female colleagues as potential sexual partners and no longer say things some women at work might find offensive. Their potential sexual partners are all on AFF. It's like a different world where they are freer to say what's on their mind. One man writes, "I avoid flirting with others except online. Online, the intention is understood. In person, things get taken the wrong way."

One man told me, "I'm a polite person by nature, and I've never been accused of giving women a hard time at work, though I know a few guys who do. Still, it can be frustrating having to be careful not to be misunderstood. The nice thing about AFF is that if, say (to put it mildly), I see a woman with beautiful eyes, I can write to her and tell her what beautiful eyes she has. If her ad says she likes receiving oral sex, I can write to her and tell her how much I enjoy giving oral sex, how much I'd like to do it to her, and even tell her what positions I'd use or tell her stories about women I've been with in the past. Now, granted, chances are she'll never reply to my message, and maybe she doesn't even like what I've written, but I'm free to write it without fearing that she'll file a suit against me. It's what people do here. It's acceptable.

"I also find that now that I'm on AFF, I'm less likely to see the women at work as body parts. Instead of noticing a low cut sweater with breasts poking out, I'm more likely to see only a colleague. I can see breasts on AFF. Why risk a comment or too-long glance at work?"

On AFF, a handsome, self-confident man of thirty with a terrific body and a well-written ad and a gold membership may find that quite a few women view his page and wink, and some women may even write to him. (This is the best way, of course, for a woman to express her interest.) He may get responses from ten percent of the women to whom he writes. Most men, though, are not so fortunate.

One thirty year old told me that in six months on AFF he had only written to ten women, but five had responded, though this led to no meetings. He said, "Short messages are not a problem as long as they have some meaning to them. I will generally respond with a message similar in length to the one sent to me. I usually put in as much effort as the other person."

New standard male members expecting the offers to pour in are certain to be disappointed, and many stop checking for messages after their first week of membership. Attractive, intelligent, successful men in their mid-forties with good photos often find that they need to write to fifty women before one replies, and they might write to a hundred or more before one actually meets with them. Writing takes time, and not everyone knows how to write. Those not willing to spend the time are unlikely to do well on AFF or similar sites.

How does one write messages that result in re-sponses? Given that one already has a well-written, interesting ad and decent photos and has taken all the personality tests and all that, how does one take the next step and write something that will lead to a reply?

There are some men who are so desperate that they decide to write, say, to every woman and cou-ple within twenty miles. They write a brief stock invitation, copy it and paste it into a message to all these people, and in one marathon session, several hundred messages have been sent. Will there be any replies? Oh, yes! There will be dozens of auto-replies that mean nothing and should be deleted without reading. Will anyone else answer? Probably not, but maybe. This is a bit like mailing a flyer to every address in a zip code. Most such flyers end up in trash cans.

There are also men who have no idea of the way to a woman's heart. It's astonishing what a large percentage of men send women or couples mes-sages of one to three sentences. There are endless complaints about this on the AFF advice columns. Some women keep collections of the most horrify-ing lines.

For example: "Yo, u r 1 hot babe. I'm HOT for u. Lets doit." Or, "Hey. I've got eight inches, and I can go for hours. Just say when." Or, "I got hard when I saw your picture. This was meant to be, baby." Most women are also not pleased by descriptions of what a man wants them to do for him.

Is it sexist to say that this is a "man thing"? Lot's of men seem to think that any woman who is on AFF because she wants sex can be seduced by using the same words that would work for them: "You. Me. Now!" Women may be on AFF for pretty much the same reason men are there, and they may be just as eager for sex, but they don't respond quite the same way men respond. Who says yes to messages like the ones above? For the most part, only other men. It seems that many men don't want to talk; they want sex. If a man wants another man, he can send out messages like these and get a good response. But it rarely works with women. They're different. Classier. Better.

Some women prefer longer messages. Some prefer shorter messages. But nearly all seem to prefer focused messages. Don't bother to send a woman a message unless you've carefully read all the information she has on her ad page. This is where you find out if you have anything in common that might catch her interest. Don't lie; don't exaggerate. But use whatever advantage you have. Sometimes it's something apparently very minor that makes a woman decide to respond to a message.

If she likes jazz and you do, too, tell her about some of your favorite concerts. If she likes anal beads and you have some experience with them, tell her. After all, most people have never tried them. If you're a heavy smoker and she's not, don't waste your time. If she writes "No married men" or "No single men," do her the courtesy of respecting her wishes. (However, if you want, you could write something like, "I know you aren't interested in married men. I just wanted to tell you how much I like your haircut. Best Wishes." No harm done and no offense given.)

If AFF says you two are 100% compatible, point that out to her. If her personality profile reveals that you two are very compatible, explain why to her. If you don't, she probably won't notice. This is your chance to hold her attention for a few extra seconds, and that time may lead her to decide to get acquainted. If she has a long profile and says something surprising at the end of it, mention that. It shows you've read it all. If there's something about her photo that you like, say so (preferably not the "dirty bits," though some women appreciate that).

Part of what you are doing here is showing the woman that you respect her; you are interested in her as a person, not merely as a sex object. (Of course, if you are in fact only interested in her as a sex object, there's a good chance that this will be evident to her, no matter what you write.) The fact is, the majority of women prefer to get to know a man a bit before having sex with him, and there's nothing wrong with that at all. Sex is better that way.

In your message, tell the woman something about yourself that she'd like to know. That sort of confidence is much appreciated. However, be careful what you say or how you say it. Lots of people have traumas in their past that have deeply affected them. These traumas are so important that people may feel a deep need to tell about them, and of course people should know. On the other hand, some of these things can make a woman decide not to meet a man. Sometimes people feel the traumas so deeply that they frighten people away when they mention them. With some things, it might be better to not say anything right away.

A woman told me recently about spending hours talking with a very nice man on the telephone and enjoying him a lot. When they finally met, just for talk, he told her that he was an alcoholic who had been dry for twelve years. When he told her about some of the rough places in his life and how close he'd come to returning to drink, he frightened her. Her father had been an alcoholic, and it had been rough on her family. She didn't want to get involved with a man who might fall off the wagon if things got tough. So she told him she wasn't going to see him again.

Many men and women on AFF have been divorced, so a divorced man should not come as a surprise, but many women are wary of men who have not yet dealt with the trauma. They are also leery of men who hate their ex-wives, who have out-of-control children, who may have been violent in the past. However, if you are an ex-con, you have a duty to tell a woman this, especially if you were convicted of a violent crime.

If you have a sexually transmitted disease and have sex with a woman without telling her, you are lower than a piece of slime. I know of only one woman on AFF who admits to having caught anything from an AFF member. She caught herpes zoster from a man who came and went without telling her he had active herpes. Her husband has not caught it, but she is stuck with it. However, this woman is so responsible that her handle actually says she is positive. "I never have sex with a man I haven't warned in advance," she told me. "They have to decide for themselves whether they want to risk it. I can always tell from the way I feel if I'm entering a contagious stage, and if I am, I cancel any meetings."

In your first message, make yourself seem interesting to the woman or couple to whom you are writing. What a woman has written about herself should help you recognize what there is about you that might interest her. Emphasize that. Show somehow that you've studied her ad. That shows that you find winning her favor important. Some people recommend that you say in your first message what you'd like to do with her sexually. Others say that is too direct, that you should only mention that sort of thing if she responds and shows some interest.

Many women who might not otherwise respond to you might respond if instead of requesting sex, you asked if you could take them out for dinner, especially if you mentioned some well-known restaurant. Or, you might offer her a ride on your motorcycle, or ask her if she'd like to walk in a nearby park, or picnic together, or visit some art museum, or visit some club (let her profile guide you). Many women are very flattered if a man on AFF is seeking companionship as well as sex or gives evidence of having a brain as well as genitals and acts as if he suspects that she has one, too. Are you thinking that this is more involvement than you want or potentially too expensive? Consider that at the least, you will be having dinner with a woman who may not agree to have sex with you, but is at least interested in sex with someone and likes talking about it. There are indeed quite a few women on AFF who only want sex. If that's all you want, be honest with yourself and with the women and write only to women who want the same thing.

You may also be thinking that all this focused writing takes a lot of time. It does. Thoroughly reading an ad and crafting a good message probably takes at least twenty minutes if the message is only a quick two or three paragraphs, and it might well take an hour. Even after hours of writing to women, a response may be a rare thing. However, this is the method most likely to work. When you write, by the way, avoid using letters instead of words, as you might with instant messaging. Read over your message before you send it and correct the spelling and punctuation. Make sure the message says what you mean to say. You may be thinking that your message should reflect the way you are. However, a great many women, even women who aren't college educated, don't want to interact with a man who seems uneducated. If that's just the way you are, sorry. That's just the way they are, too. You might try writing only to women with several obvious errors in their ads. There are quite a few of them to choose from.

Now that you understand how hard it is to get a woman to respond to your message and how few men get responses, if you do get a response, you can feel really good about yourself. (On AFF and most similar sites, there are a few women who will do a man the courtesy to write back and say "No, thanks; I don't think we're compatible," but they are rare. The excuse women give is, "If I wrote 'no, thanks' to all the men who write to me, it would take two hours a day." We should have such troubles, eh?

Even if you never meet, getting a few responses will build your self-esteem. As your self-esteem improves, so does your confidence. Women are far more likely to choose a confident man.

But getting a message back is not the same as a meeting. Once a woman responds to you, you need to begin developing a relationship by getting to know her. Tell her about yourself, yes, but even better, ask her questions about herself. Base your questions on her profile if you can. Ask about things she's likely to know about. Some people do not want to give details about their lives, but others do. A relationship develops best in an atmosphere of trust. You may find yourselves gradually revealing more and more about yourselves as you learn to trust each other.

Photos are a part of trust. Most AFF members don't have photos of themselves on their ad pages, but they are doing themselves a disservice. Many people have face photos or clothed photos but no nude photos. Others have nude photos but no face photos. Whichever you have on your ad, when you send your first message you should send a face photo and a full body photo, clothed or not. You may be thinking that you don't want to trust your face to someone you don't know who will probably not respond. But why would you entrust your penis to a woman without sharing your face with her?

A woman would be crazy to meet with a guy who won't show his face to her or says he doesn't have any photos of himself. This is not because she should hold out for someone handsome (women have many definitions of attractiveness), but because sensitive, insightful people can read people's faces and find in them signs of danger, kindness, warmth, cruelty, arrogance, or confidence. So show her your face. If you can't trust people that much or if you are too much of a public figure, then you probably should avoid AFF and similar sites.

There are no definite rules regarding when or how to meet. Some women are eager to meet as soon as possible. Some want to exchange several messages or e-mails. Some want to talk on the phone. Some women want to meet in a public place first with no promise of anything else. Other women will happily welcome men to their home for a first meeting. Some women will string out e-mails for months with promises of meetings, yet never meet.

One man told me, "There was this woman who answered my first message, and we began corresponding. We lived about ninety minutes apart, but she wouldn't tell me her address. Finally we met and went to an afternoon movie. She insisted that I meet her in a gas station parking lot, and she wouldn't ride in my car—she had to drive. We got on quite well. I didn't try to kiss her. I invited her out to dinner. Now a year has passed, but we have yet to meet again. We set up the dinner date, but she cancelled it. Over and over. She sends me messages saying I'm the dearest friend she has, her only close friend. Close friend! I've spent two hours with her!

"I finally told her this wasn't working, that it was silly to call me her dearest friend when she wouldn't even give me her address, so I thought we'd better call it off. She sent me her address and apologized. Now I hear from her about once a month, and we talk about meeting and set things up, but I know we'll never meet. I'm just being polite."

Most women aren't this way, but many do make it clear that they reserve the right to eat and run, to meet once with no physical contact, then say, "Never again." This may be disappointing to most men, but it's a fair request.

It shouldn't be necessary to mention this, but before you go to see a woman, make sure you are scrupulously clean everywhere. Don't show up in worn jeans and a t-shirt, even if that's the way you usually dress. She'll probably appreciate your trying to look your best for her. Bring her flowers, maybe a dozen roses or two. It's amazing how many women have never received roses. You might think this is merely a way to seduce a woman, but it is a pleasure to give a woman something she deserves, something that will please her. And, of course, it does work!

Be polite. Open doors for her. Pull back her chair for her. Ask her advice. Listen to it. When you are talking, ask her about herself. Women are often much better at getting men to talk than men are at getting women to talk, but try. Ask specific questions that might yield interesting answers. Talk about sex is okay, but keep it light-hearted. Don't brag about all your old girlfriends or your sexual capabilities.

I won't try to tell you what to do after that. That's up to you. If you are both in the mood and it's meant to be, you'll figure it out. But whatever you do, when you get home, send her an e-mail or call her and say thank you.

What are sites such as AFF like for women? Despite some frustrations, the women I've asked have generally been very positive. Many women seem to join such sites with no intention of actually meeting anyone. Some who join merely want to flirt. Often these women love sex, but they are cautious. They enjoy pornography; they enjoy talk about sex; but perhaps they are married or not eager to get into a serious relationship or worried about the danger of having sex with a number of partners. Perhaps they focus on the Magazine and read and write advice. Perhaps they prefer exchanging e-mails or instant messages. One woman told me, "It's fun to get messages, and it's much safer. You never know who men really are, but they don't know my name, address, and phone number, so I can exchange messages without danger. Sometimes the messages are friendly. Sometimes they are pretty hot. It's nice to have acquaintances who keep me in their thoughts."

Some women don't plan to meet anyone, but they find they can't resist. "The idea of sex online sort of embarrassed me," one woman wrote. "Exchanging messages seemed pleasanter, and I could write and read things and smile or laugh without blushing. The thing is, some of the messages were pretty hot. Eventually I broke down and began meeting guys. I wish I hadn't waited so long."

Some women join looking for a special long-term relationship or a husband, but fail to find quite what they are looking for. There are men on AFF who want or say they want lasting relationships, but they don't necessarily want them with the women who answer their messages.

There are plenty of women online who are exhibitionists. They enjoy being seen. Some of these post photos on their ad pages and send more photos to those who ask for them. This can be quite satisfying. A small but growing number are using webcams. A woman toying with herself on a webcams. A woman toying with herself on a webcam can easily draw hundreds of viewers at once, even if she is fifty-five and a hundred pounds over-weight. For true exhibitionists, this is very pleas-ant.

One of the most useful things about sites such as AFF is the way they can increase women's self-esteem. If a woman is on AFF, men feel free to write and tell her what they think. Generally these are things they would not dare to say in an office, on the street, or on the factory floor. Granted, they may flatter, they may exaggerate, and they may lie. Nevertheless, many men truly do admire a wide variety of shapes, and without doubt a large number of those who write will be honest in their admiration.

The comments of the woman I'm about to quote are similar to comments I have heard from many women. "I'm forty-five, 5'5", and I weigh 180 pounds. I used to weigh 220, but I was able to lose quite a bit. Still, I felt fat at 180, and I knew I looked fat. My arms were fat, my belly rolled over my underwear, my breasts hung way down, and I had a double chin. I felt pretty ugly. Of course, even when I was slimmer, I was never a beauty.

"But I was also lonely, though, and I'd done without ice cream for months and spent hours at the gym. I decided to treat myself to an AFF silver membership, just to look around. I tried to honestly describe what I look like and what I like to do. I had my sister take some digital photos of me, and I put a couple of those on my ad: a face shot and a clothed photo of me leaning against a tree (and nearly as big around).

"I didn't know what to expect, but I was sort of hoping I might get three or four messages from interested men. When I got home from work the next night, I went online to have a look. To my amazement, I had eighty-three responses. I couldn't believe it. I couldn't remember the last time anyone said anything nice about my looks. I assumed this was because I was fat and ugly.

"Some of the responses were nasty, brutish, and short. I deleted them without a response. Some had amazing photos worth saving. Some had photos that made me laugh (but that's not nice). Lots of men said very nice things about me, and often they seemed to mean it. Sometimes they complimented me about strange things I never notice, like the shape of my ears or my fingers. Sometimes they mentioned that I looked like a really nice person, just the sort of woman they most like. Sometimes they wrote about their love for fat women. I'd never actually considered that there might be men who prefer fat women. That was an interesting concept. Could it be true?

"Some men sent photos, and some of them were quite attractive. Others weren't. Some of the men wrote rather scary things. They were deleted. Others wrote funny things. Some wrote rather interesting messages. I spent several hours answering messages. It was the most fun I'd had in years.

"The number of new responses decreased as the days passed, but I was still getting half a dozen messages from new men a day, plus messages from various men with whom I'd begun corresponding. Meanwhile, a strange thing started happening. At first when men would compliment me, I'd think, "That's a lie!" or "They're just buttering me up." Sometimes I'd blush. As the days passed, though, and I kept reading all these compliments, I stopped denying them. I gradually started accepting them at face value. Then I started seeing myself as an attractive woman, bit by bit. I started looking in the mirror more and liking what I saw a bit better. I started standing straighter, walking more confidently. I went shopping for some more attractive and less shapeless clothes. I got a more stylish haircut. As I gained confidence, a weird thing happened. I started getting compliments at work, and in the course of a month two men actually asked me out!

"I finally met some men in person. I won't tell you all the details. Suffice it to say that I was sure they would hate my body, but they loved it and let me know it. At first I didn't want them to see me with the light on. Soon, though, I was parading myself in front of them, showing off, and boy did it do wonders for my ego when I saw the sight of my body make them hard. I feel like a new person, and I really like that person."

As with men, photos are important. A woman without photos will still get some responses, but she will get enormously more messages with photos. The quality of the photos has some impact on what sort of man responds, too. Unless a woman with no photos writes a really warm, sexy, welcoming profile, she may tend to draw the more hard-up of the men. A face shot and a nude shot may draw different sorts of men, but there will still be a lot of overlap.

Some women only have clothed shots. Others only have nudes with no faces. Some have both. Actually, all of these options can be successful. However, there is a wide range in the quality of the photos. Some photos make women look much less attractive than they are. These should be avoided. Sometimes webcam shots are adequate, but they are seldom ideal. It's important for a woman to remind her photographer that raising the camera a bit above eye level makes a woman look slimmer. So does a close-up taken with a moderately telephoto lens. Natural daylight lighting is generally more attractive than flash. The effort it takes to get it right pays off in quality of contacts.

If possible, a woman should have more than one photo. Women who are gold or silver paid members are likely to be "real." Women with three or four photos are more likely to be considered "real," as well, so they get more serious responses. The ideal photos are well-composed, well-lighted, and attractive, but they aren't studio photos with studio lighting. They are honest—they look like the people—but they look like the people at their best. Nude shots are nice but not necessary. Face shots and clothed body shots are better than nudes without a face (at least when it comes to getting quality responses). Any photos are more effective than no photos, given that most men don't bother to look at ads without photos.

There is a temptation for people, especially women, to lie about their age on sites such as AFF. This is understandable, and if they look younger than their age and list themselves as a couple years younger than they are, there's not much harm done. The sad fact is that AFF allows people to search ads by age. Women are likely to list as their upper age limit men ten years older than themselves, but men are likely to list women no older than themselves, so they may not view women who are a year or two older. There is also a sort of psychological barrier at the age of fifty. Many people willing to consider a person of forty-nine will balk at a person of fifty. They may limit their search to people forty-nine or younger.

The thing is, there are AFF members in their fifties who are better lovers and in better shape than many members in their twenties and thirties, and there are some in their sixties who are better in bed than many in their forties. What's a woman to do if she's fifty-five and knows she is entirely capable of satisfying a man of forty-five, but knows he's unlikely to notice her? She should lie! She should list herself as, say, forty-five or forty-nine within the Physical Information search criteria. Then, on her profile, she should write, say, "Actually, I am a young, attractive, and hot fifty-five year old woman, but I know lots of great guys don't search that high. So here I am, and here you are. Do you like what you see? All my parts still work. What are you going to do about it?"

On the other hand, there are women who claim to be fifty-five when their face photo says they are sixty-five. Worse is the woman who claims an age much younger than she looks but has only photos that don't show her clearly. A man may be willing to date an older woman, but be uncomfortable about one who lies about herself. One man said, "I found this woman with one attractive but blurry photo who claimed to be fifty-one, 5'2", and athletic. We exchanged e-mails and liked each other. We talked for hours on the phone and had a good

time, though her voice sounded sort of old. I wondered when she talked about having a ten year relationship with a show biz personality I know is
eighty-five. When we finally met, it turned out
that she was actually sixty-two, 4'9", and fifty
pounds overweight, wearing a very short minidress.
Maybe she was once athletic, but she couldn't
climb a short flight of stairs without stopping at
the top to pant, and I couldn't walk slowly enough
for her to keep up with me. I took her to a nice
concert, but when she needed to use the restroom,
she insisted on taking the elevator rather than the
stairs. But she couldn't hold her bladder, and in
this fancy elevator urine poured down her fish-net
nylons, filled her shoes, and flooded the carpeted
floor! I was polite, but we were both too embarrassed to meet again."

There is also a temptation for women to fudge
the facts regarding their size. If they have body
photos on their ad, this isn't too serious. It can be
amusing, though, to note how subjectively people
use the terms available. On AFF, women can list
their size as average, slim/petite, athletic, ample,
a few extra pounds, or large. Apparently these
terms are open to discussion, and they seem to reveal either self-esteem or wishful thinking. I've
seen women list themselves as having "a few extra
pounds" who are a hundred pounds heavier than the
National Institutes of Health recommendations

(http://www.nhlbisupport.com/bmi/bmicalc.htm;
retrieved 1 March 2006). I've also seen women list
themselves as having "a few extra pounds" who
have a six-pack abdomen but also have five pounds
more on their hips than they want. I've seen women
list themselves as "large" who are within the NIH
recommendations for normal weight. Some list
themselves as "athletic" because they go to a gym
once a week, even though they are overweight. Average seems to mean an average of thirty pounds
overweight.

Many men on AFF and similar sites complain
that they write to many women, but virtually none
show the common courtesy of writing back to say
"No, thank-you," even though there are stock responses available on AFF that make this nearly as
fast as deleting a message. Those few women who
do bother to reply to say no may frequently get a
follow-up message such as this: "Thank-you for
writing to say you weren't interested. Even though
you aren't interested, your message means a lot.
I've written to maybe 200 women in the past few
months, and you are the only one who has responded." There, now doesn't that make you feel
good about yourself? Spreading joy and sunshine
wherever you go!

When women begin corresponding with men on
AFF or similar sites, trust is a big question. Should
they reveal their last name? Their address? Their

e-mail address? Their telephone number? In the age of Google, any of these bits of information may reveal the others, along with other less expected data. One woman revealed her home phone number and was surprised when her new sexual partner was able to converse about scientific papers her husband had published and various law suits he had filed and was even able to discuss reviews of films her daughter had written for a newspaper. The partner did not misuse this information, but she hadn't realized what was out there.

Some women are tempted to use phony names, but this can backfire. It's easier to use their actual first names, and often they won't need to reveal their last names unless they want to. Cell phone numbers don't reveal addresses (along with maps and aerial photos of the home).

Probably if people are meeting for sex, they should be willing to trust each other. If they can't, then perhaps they shouldn't be meeting. Still, at swing clubs people often meet as friends for years without knowing last names.

Women are sometimes urged to never meet in their home men they don't know well. They are told that they should first meet at a coffee shop, bar, restaurant, bookstore, or something of the sort—someplace public. Then they should talk for a few hours. Then they should decide whether they want to meet again. This is a prudent approach, though it is not the fast way to satisfaction. Some women have a "no sex on the first date" policy and even put this in their profile. They still have many offers.

However, there are plenty of women who do give men their addresses, and the men come to their home, and everything goes fine, year after year. It would be fair for a woman to say that she will give her address and phone number, but only if he gives her his. This way she can check up on him before their meeting. A married man, say, who reveals his home phone number and address is very unlikely to be abusive, given that his partner can hold this information over his head.

The horror stories I've heard about meetings have been of disappointments rather than danger. One woman told me of a man coming to her house, having sex with her, then asking for directions to the nearest drugstore with long hours. She asked if he needed more condoms—she had a supply. No, he wanted to get her a surprise, and he'd be back in a few minutes. He never returned.

Another woman corresponded for months with a man who lived eight hours away. Finally they met at a nice hotel halfway in between. They were planning to spend the weekend together, but at 2 a.m. the man told her he had to leave early to go home? Was it something she did or didn't do? He finally revealed that he didn't think much of her oral sex skills. Of course, he himself hadn't given her any oral sex.

More common are the stories of being stood up. It seems that most women who have met several men on AFF have a story about waiting at a bar or restaurant for hours, then going home alone and embittered and feeling worthless. It seems amazing that given how hard it is for men to get a woman to agree to meet, any would fail to show up, but it seems that quite a few chicken out. In some cases, the women later discover that the man showed up and watched them for a while, then left. This is hard to bear. Of course, there are plenty of women who have stood up men, too.

Meeting for the first time can be wonderfully exciting, but it can also be uncomfortable. When people go on regular dates, they may be wondering if anything sexual will happen, and that adds a certain piquancy to the evening. It is somewhat different, however, when both people know that unless something goes wrong, there will be sex for dessert. It both makes things easier and makes things harder. There's less likelihood of misunderstandings and hurt feelings. If a man fumbles toward that first kiss, he knows the woman is not going to slap him and say, "For shame! I'm not that kind of girl."

Many correspondents say that there is a rather interesting psychological ballet that goes on. The evening wears on; conversations fall silent. Does one of you say, "Shall we go to my place"? Does the woman say, "Do you have condoms?" Perhaps there's the old standby of kissing in the living room until people rip each other's clothes off. Time keeps ticking away. Perhaps the man or the woman stands up and says, "Unless you want me to stop, I'm taking off my clothes." This is an excellent ice-breaker. It can also lead to an amusingly connubial round of trips to the bathroom and brushing of teeth. (This connubiality is a substantial difference between the middle-aged dating of AFF members and the fumblings of adolescents.)

Often the first meeting is wonderfully romantic, exciting, and sexual. This is the sort of meeting that makes it worthwhile. It's best in one's own home, but even a motel can be nice.

The big question is if you will meet again. Many women prefer a single meeting, and many who thought they would prefer a longer relationship come to prefer a shorter relationship. One woman writes, "When I wrote my profile, I stressed that I was looking for one good man who would be my lover for a long time. I was happy with my husband, more or less, except that we haven't had sex in years, and I thought it would be nice to have a lover I could count on.

"The first few men I met with—truth be told— were not very good lovers, for various reasons. (A lot of men really are astonishingly bad in bed, even AFF men.) None of them seemed very interested in sticking around, and I couldn't well encourage them. I did meet a man I got along with pretty well, and we've remained friends for months, but he's ten years older than me and just not very sexually inclined, and we've only kissed a little. I've had a couple good lovers who stuck around for a couple months. One of them appreciated all my little kinks and was wildly satisfying.

"But the odd thing is, although I meant to find one long-term lover, I now find that I really prefer meeting a man just once or twice. The novelty of it is exciting. The hunt and the verbal foreplay by e-mail excites me. Getting to know people is exciting. I have a husband for long-term. Even the lover who was very satisfying sort of got old after a couple months of weekly meetings in tawdry motels. So now I tend toward quantity rather than quality, though quality is nice, too."

Despite this report, many women do prefer a long-term relationship, and some of them find it. But women looking for this are likely to be disappointed a few times, and it may take a couple years before they find what they want. Meanwhile, they won't find what they want unless they test men out.

Some women (and many couples) deliberately exclude married men. There are sound reasons why this is a good idea. (There are also sound reasons why men should avoid married women.) Married men are less often available. If they are happily married, they are not about to leave their wives. If they are unhappily married, it is not fun to be caught up in divorce proceedings—it tends to be a very tense time. Married men are not free to share their lives as thoroughly as single men. They may not be able to comfortably be seen in public with a lover. Some suffer from guilt feelings. If a woman comes to care deeply for a married man, her life is not easy.

On the other hand, a married lover is sometimes a good choice. He may be stable, normal, solid in a satisfying way. He's less likely to want to move in or move a woman across the country. For a woman who wants sex only once a week or once or twice a month or who likes to sleep alone, a married man may be ideal. He may be likewise ideal for a woman who only wants sex and not a life with a man. It may also be that married men are more likely to be free of disease. Many married men want multiple partners, of course, but many more are quite happy with a pleasant afternoon of sex with the same woman now and then.

All told, internet sex and swinger sites can be an excellent way for people who want sex to meet each other. What seems unsatisfactory about

them for many men and women might be quite satisfying to others. Some find their needs met by
looking at ads, others by contributing to advice
columns, others by messaging, and others by
webcam exhibitionism and/or voyeurism.

Those who want to meet people can generally
achieve their aim with work. Men will probably need
to send out hundreds of carefully tailored messages to get a few partners. Women can get partners just by choosing among those who send messages. Braver ones are more likely to get what they
want by writing directly to people without waiting
for them to indicate an interest.

While I've devoted little space here to couples
and even less to men seeking men or women seeking
women, the techniques are the same. The difference between a woman seeking a man and a woman
seeking a woman is a matter of taste and orientation. Similarly, some people want to meet with couples or groups. What we desire or what we are
comfortable with depends to a large extent on not
only our orientation, but on the formative influences in our past and our current tastes and situations.

Some people want to meet for what some call
"vanilla sex." Others may have kinkier tastes, such
as bondage, domination, or subservience. Some
prefer vinyl, some leather, and some (both men and
women) stockings and high heels. There are some

kinks that don't seem to have much to do with sex. Many do, though, and whether or not we ourselves are interested, why need we forbid others to break their "mind-forged manacles"?

AdultFriendFinder and similar sites are about freedom, exploration, not about being limited by tradition or cultural taboos. Members limit themselves according to what is healthy or not, what is safe or not, what hurts others and what does not. Thus, membership is ideally rational, reasoning out do and don't. It develops an experimental and experiential knowledge of right and wrong, rather than quietly but grudgingly doing as told.

Chapter 2:
Having Fun at Swing Clubs

Okay, you've been on AdultFriendFinder for a couple years. You've met a number of people and had some great experiences. You think you know what fun is. Then you meet someone who wants to take you to a swing club. You don't really know what a swing club is, but you have an idea, and it sounds tawdry, scary, cheapening—not your sort of place at all. Your friend insists that he or she thought the same before trying it out and that if you would only try it, you'd love it. Would you? What should you expect? Let me tell you.

There are more than 500 heterosexual swing clubs of various sorts in the United States (SwingLifeStyle claims to list "a total of 1095 verified clubs"). Some have their own premises. Others meet in hotels or bars (these are often called "Meet and Greets"). California has more than 100. Florida, New York, and Texas each have more than 60. Half the states have at least ten. Only three states have none listed with my source (www.swinglifestyle.com).

The popularity of swing clubs goes back to 1975, when Plato's Retreat opened in New York. Swinging house parties have been with us for millennia (see the ruins of Pompeii for examples), but Plato's Retreat introduced people to the idea of paying to be in a club where most people were there to have sex with each other. At its height, Plato's Retreat had 1,000 participants some nights.

One might expect it to have been, like such popular New York dance venues as Club 54, very exclusive, limited to "the beautiful people." Certainly many famous people visited. However, it also drew large numbers of working class and middle class people within driving distance of New York. Plato's Retreat closed down in 1985. (There's an interesting history of Plato's Retreat by Jon Hart in Russ Kick's *Everything You Know About Sex Is Wrong*.)

Few clubs today ever have more than a couple hundred participants (many have only a dozen show up some nights), and they vary widely in their interests and rules. A few focus on BBWs or on racial diversity or racial exclusivity. Some draw mostly working class people, while others draw primarily the wealthy. Some have members mostly in their 20s and 30s, while others have members mostly in their 30s, 40s, and 50s. There is a wide variation in friendliness or cliquishness. There's a big variation in cost and amenities. It's hard to describe a representative club.

Those who have attended a few clubs know what they are like and whether or not they like them. Some are temperamentally suited for them, and some are not. Some love them and some don't (though those who don't may have gone to the wrong club). However, many readers who have never been to a club will appreciate information on what a swing club is like at its best, or at least one way a swing club can be when it's a good one, so let's visit one from the Mid-West. We'll call it the Candy Store because many AFF members visiting it would feel like kids in a candy store with five dollars to spend. I'm going to give more details than many people will want because I always feel more comfortable going somewhere new if I know a lot about it in advance.

Some people at the Candy Store have been going there for years and have never been to any other club. As one woman said, "When you've found a place that feels like home, why go elsewhere?" Actually, the Candy Store doesn't seem at all like most homes, but apart from that, I can understood her position.

Like many clubs, the Candy Store is out in the country on a property zoned as "commercial." It is pleasant, not spotless but clean enough, and not very glitzy. The directions aren't on the web site. Directions are sent after you join. New members are told to arrive at 7:30 so they can be given a tour.

Like many swing clubs, the Candy Store is BYOB—the club doesn't have a liquor license, but members can bring their own bottles, and there are bartenders to serve the drinks. Non-alcoholic drinks are provided free.

Ready for your tour? You are met at the gate by a large, muscular man, asked for your reservation number, checked off on a clipboard, and directed to a parking spot. The management doesn't want unexpected people arriving. You walk in carrying a bottle of wine or a six-pack of beer or something similar, along with a bag with any necessaries such as sexy clothes, lube, and condoms. You show your ID (yes, your real name will be on file), fill out paperwork, fork over some cash, and sign a paper swearing you aren't a journalist doing an exposé or a law enforcement agent (cops can join, but they have to fill out a special form).

As in many swing clubs, the nightly charge for members is different for couples, single women, and single men, signaling their relative scarcity. This night couples pay $30, single women a dollar, and single men $50. Other nights it is higher. Some clubs charge $100 or more for single men. Some charge $100 per couple.

The rules posted online state that at the Candy Store, single bi females are at the top of the pecking order and single men at the bottom. They just have to grin and bear it. Many clubs do not allow single men at all. Others admit no more single men than there are single women signed up. Some count the total number of women who sign up, then admit two single men for every ten women. Many clubs control the number of single men by charging them a lot of money. This does help increase the likelihood that only the more prosperous single men will get in. However, given that it isn't hard for a single man to spend $50 at a dance club trying to pick up women, the Candy Store seems like a pretty fair deal.

After you pay, you are given a tour by a pair of volunteer hosts. You start off in the main room. There are perhaps forty tables for four grouped around a twenty-foot square hardwood dance floor with lots of flashing lights. There is a stage with a brass pole for pole dancing. There is a booth for the DJ. Throughout the night he will play dance hits from the past thirty years, including a number of recent rap songs. Some of the songs will have adult lyrics. Among the favorites—played every night—will be "Save a Horse, Ride a Cowboy" and "Play that Funky Music, White Boy." There is a U-shaped bar. You leave your bottle with a bartender, and a number is written on the bottle and on your name tags. (This system actually works quite smoothly, and the written numbers are handy when the music is loud—just point at your number and hold up fingers for the number of drinks.)

Then you move on to the rest of the club. There is a room with a couple pool tables and a couple couches and another large room with couches for conversation. There is a unisex locker room, a men's room, a women's room, and a unisex shower room with two shower stalls big enough for two.

Down a hallway are several rooms with lockable doors but windows allowing people to observe the action within. Another hallway has rooms with lockable doors and windows with curtains or no windows at all, for those who want a bit more privacy. (Some people enjoy being watched, while others can't function when others are watching.) Some rooms have one double bed, others two.

In an annex are rooms without doors. Anyone is welcome to come in and watch or, if permitted, join in. Later in the night, perhaps, you will watch the woman giving you the tour in one of these rooms as she uses a strap-on dildo on another woman while a dozen men stand around watching.

A final hallway leads to a variety of specialty rooms. Two rooms have sex swings where women can sit, legs spread, while others have their way with them. These swings are on electrical hoists controlled by buttons so the height can be adjusted just right. Two rooms have gynecology tables with foot stirrups (sorry, but you have to bring your own rubber gloves and instruments). A couple rooms are set up with padded wrist and ankle restraints for those interested in bondage (there are some whips on the walls, but they are screwed and glued and for display only). One room has an actual jail cell in the middle of it (bring your own prisoner and guard).

One room with two double beds is lighted only by a string of dark blue lights, and these can be unplugged. The rule for this room is that anyone playing here can be touched at will, and, of course, in the dark, one wouldn't know who was touching whom. (Sounds like fun, but you may never manage to find the room occupied.)

All of these rooms have tissues and towels (some clubs also provide condoms in every room). There are also attendants whose job is to quickly change the sheets between room uses and make sure the rules are followed.

Another large room contains two hot tubs, each big enough for at least a dozen strangers or a couple dozen close friends. Fresh towels are provided.

A large sign at the door reads, "Please do not cum in the hot tub." This rule is not always followed, but you will probably never see coagulated sperm floating around.

As one might expect in a place with a number of single men, voyeurism is common. The rules are spelled out carefully. If there's a window, you may watch. If the door is open, you may enter. Do not touch anyone without asking. If you are told "No," then stop whatever you are doing. If you are asked to leave, then leave. Don't make rude comments, laugh, or discuss sports (et cetera) while watching people play. The price of admission does not guarantee that you will get to play with someone.

Eating food is nearly as important as drinking in many clubs. The Candy Store has a dining area with a couple dozen tables for four. There is a chef and a full buffet every night, not large but adequate, with food that is marginally edible. This is included in the cost of admission. (Indeed, apart from bringing your own bottle and maybe tipping the bartender a couple dollars, everything is included in the admission price.)

By the time you've finished the tour, the club is starting to fill up. Attendance ranges from a very light night with about 100 people to New Year's Eve with perhaps 250.

What sort of people frequent the Candy Store? Nearly everyone seems to be between thirty and sixty. There are a few people in their twenties and a few in their sixties. Probably not more than 10% of the people would be considered slim or athletic. Most range from thirty or forty pounds extra, up (according to the government height/weight ratios). Comfortable-looking people. Definitely, people who are not fond of larger men and women would find slim pickings at the Candy Store. The age range and size range is different in some clubs. At some, perhaps 90% are slim or athletic.

It seems to you that those at the Candy Store are predominantly working class, along with a good percentage of middle class people and a handful of professionals. Many work in factories, warehouses, and offices. They build houses, drive trucks, and put out fires. They look just like the people you see at the mall on Sunday afternoon. This is the heart of America.

Probably the majority of people who visit the Candy Store are regulars who show up at least once a month. Some come weekly. Your general impression will probably be that these are nice, ordinary, friendly people. They are eager to meet new members and to like those who are willing to like them.

At least among members, the Candy Store has a reputation for being one of the friendliest clubs in the country. Some people drive three hundred miles or more to visit the Candy Store when they can. If you come with a friend who is a regular and can introduce you to friends, you will do well, but most new members find it pretty easy to meet people. Yes, of course, plenty of people won't look at those they don't already know and act as if the people are invisible, but that usually changes once they are introduced. There are also plenty of stories about people who tried several clubs and felt unaccepted before discovering the Candy Store.

So, you are interested in visiting, but you are wondering what you should wear? The web site warns visitors to dress to impress. What does that mean in actuality? Very few men wear jeans (in many clubs jeans are not allowed). A few men wear suits or even tuxedoes. Some wear colored t-shirts. Many wear polo shirts, Hawaiian shirts, or button-down shirts with slacks. Perhaps not all that impressive, in general.

For women, dress seems to run from sexy to slutty, and there is always an element of irony to it, as if the women might look in the mirror, see themselves, and burst out laughing. They are having fun wearing costumes. (It's no wonder that there are frequent "dress-up" nights like Halloween and Valentine's Day, or pajama night, thong night, toga night, or sexy underwear night.)

Here's a woman dancing in a mini-skirt so short that you can see two inches of her cheeks. There's a woman in a tight red party dress and spike heels.

Here's a woman dressed in black vinyl. There's a woman in fishnet nylons, garter belt, heels, and a black lace corset with both cheeks exposed. Here's a woman wearing a sexy, floor-length nightgown. There's a woman in a babydoll nightgown. Black seems to be the most popular color, followed by red. (There are other clubs where women seem more likely to wear white or pastels, but sexy is definitely expected.) Few women wear long pants, business suits, or modest clothing, but those aren't forbidden.

Around the bar, in the dining room, and on the dance floor, people are more or less clothed. They aren't supposed to walk around nude. However, it's quite common for a woman to pull out her breasts and dance around that way. There are lots of glimpses. Once in awhile people get carried away. After midnight, things are allowed to get a bit looser.

As one might expect, the dance floor is a great place to meet people at the Candy Store. First time visitors wear a red name tag and get extra attention. At 10:00 there is a much-loved Get Acquainted Dance, with the DJ ordering everyone to change partners every minute. Unlike the usual dance club, it's quite acceptable to fondle the breasts and buttocks of a dance partner you've never met before, and an erection is considered a compliment and groped with pleasure. Kisses are exchanged freely and deeply as part of the fun. If a single guy has his wits about him, by 10:05 he can make a couple friends who want to see more of him.

Here are a few things you will never see at the Candy Store. Unlike many dance clubs, you will never see any "professional" women trying to peddle themselves. You will never see any drug use (apart from Viagra). You'll see plenty of tipsiness, but very little drunkenness—much less than at the average bar on any night. You are unlikely to ever see a fight or even an argument. (Frankly, I'd much rather have a swing club on my block than a bar. It's quiet outside, self-policed, safe, and drunk drivers aren't much of a problem.)

As one might expect, at the Candy Store people eye each other and wonder about availability, but there is a huge difference between the Candy Store and a disco or singles' bar. At a dance club, the ability to seduce is crucial (unless you are unusually handsome or beautiful), and with seduction comes calculation, exaggeration, and lying, pretending to be what you aren't. A guy who meets a girl is constantly trying to figure out if she is available sexually and how she might be convinced to accept him as a partner. She's wondering if he'll still like her in the morning. People grow increasingly desperate to find a partner as the night nears its end. If one man tries to horn in on another man's choice, a fight may erupt. Men are trying to get women drunk. Men are drinking to get the courage to approach someone new.

The Candy Store is wildly different. At least 95% of the people are there because they are admitted lovers of sex, whether or not they want to play that night. Most are very willing to have one or more partners in the course of the evening, and they don't need much convincing. Those who don't want another partner at least know where they are, so they aren't offended when people ask and aren't afraid to say no. The result is that there is very little pressure. There is very little seduction necessary, and the seduction is fun.

Instead, both men and women are asking themselves, "Does this seem like a nice person? Is this person pleasant to look at? Are any alarm bells ringing? Can I imagine being aroused by this person for an hour?" There is such a big difference between seducing a man or woman who might somehow end up as your life partner and choosing to spend a pleasant hour with a person when you know you'll be going home with the significant other you love and live with. If there is no chemistry between people, it doesn't matter—they aren't required to get together. There will be chemistry with someone else. And if not, there will be next week.

The separation of sex from the implicit or explicit violence of seduction is both refreshing and relaxing. It seems healthy, natural, the way we were meant to be.

Some couples only play with each other. Some couples only play with other couples—no singles. Most actually exchange partners (full swap). Others may play around with the other couples, but only have intercourse with their spouses (soft swap). Some couples split off and play as singles, whether for an hour or the evening. Some men and women are uncomfortable playing with another partner if their own spouse is present. Others feel that the spouse should always be present. There's a lot of variation, and it is all acceptable. There may be the occasional couple that is offended when you say, "My wife and I only have intercourse with each other," but most will accept that, even if it doesn't interest them. In the Candy Store, there's plenty for all, or at least most.

One of the rules at the Candy Store is that it is generally impolite for a single guy to approach a woman directly. If he wants to dance with her and she is sitting with her husband, he should ask her husband for permission. If he wants to take her away to play for a while, he should again ask permission (or perhaps she will ask). The same goes for a woman who wants to go off with someone else's husband. Courtesy is always appreciated.

What people say when they've been talking for a few minutes or an hour and are feeling willing is often "Would you like to get a room?" This is a non-threatening approach, and it's easy to say, "I don't think so" or "Let me ask my husband."

The most common word for sex at the Candy Store is "playing." People may say, "Would you like to play?" or "Have you played with anyone tonight?" Playing is actually a wonderful term for what goes on at the Candy Store. Playing is fun, it's a game, it's recreation, it's non-threatening, and it's safe.

Considering that many couples have sex with each other before leaving for the Candy Store for the evening or play with several partners in the course of the evening, it's not surprising that erectile dysfunction is very common. Some men turn to Viagra as a solution to this problem, but erectile dysfunction is still very much in evidence.

Perhaps there is a hot foursome going on in a room without a door, and there are several men standing around watching. Perhaps several of them have unzipped and pulled out their penises. It's quite likely that not one of them will have an erection.

Here's a beautiful women on a bed with a man of 55. It's clear that they are fond of each other. Perhaps they've done this several times in the past year. She has to use her oral talents to bring him to erection, and despite her lovely body, she may have to stop a couple times to get him up again.

Here's a guy in a room with another man and a woman to attempt a double penetration—a feat he's been looking forward to for a month. As he rolls on a condom he wilts, and nothing he does will raise the dead.

This is so very common that it's almost a surprise when a man has an orgasm. Many will play with several women in the course of an evening, having an erection all or part of the time with each, without ever reaching a climax. Of course, there are many men who are finished for the night and no longer interested as soon as they have had an orgasm. Then they go to the bar and have a beer or two while their partners seek out the guys who are still hard and eager. Those men are very popular later in the evening.

Women may also get orgasmed out. Many of the women at the Candy Store who are generally multi-orgasmic may find that even though they are in wildly exciting situations, they are not having orgasms. Quite possibly they have simply been as excited as they can be for the time being.

This is why the concept of play and playing at the Candy Store is so liberating. Men don't have to be embarrassed if they lose their erections because their partner assumes that they have already striven manfully with someone else in the course of the evening. Women are free to enjoy kissing, tasting, insertion without feeling that they have to "satisfy" their partners. They are free to say to a man, "That was wonderful, but I don't think I'll be able to come again tonight." He won't be offended.

This concept of playing and play is perhaps the most exciting thing swing clubs like the Candy Store have to offer. We are so accustomed to sex being a process of excitation leading to orgasm. It is so liberating to see it, instead, as people enjoying each other physically, mentally, and emotionally, touching and tasting, stroking, hugging, kissing. It is so refreshing to be able to laugh together, to smile. It is so relaxing when a woman says, "Let's just play—I'm all orgasmed out," or when a man says, "I really have no need to come—let's just touch." Sex as play opens men and women to a wonderful new level of relationship.

Another aspect of this relationship is the apparent lack of jealousy. I'm sure there is jealousy here and there, but much less than in many marriages where nothing is going on. A man who is enjoying a woman he's recently met is less likely to be jealous as he watches his wife enjoying that woman's husband. A couple soon learns to jettison jealousy when what they know for certain is that they enjoy others, but they love only each other and will be going home together. They will soon be in each other's arms recounting the evening's exploits.

Probably half the women at the Candy Store are comfortable playing with other women, but there's no pressure to do so. Sometimes this is in the context of playing as a threesome or foursome, but sometimes as a couple. Some women are comfortable kissing other women's mouths, but nothing else. Some women will kiss another woman's breasts, but not her mouth. Some are willing to receive oral sex from another woman but not give it. Women know their comfort zone, and that's fine. If they feel excited enough to step outside it, that's okay, too.

By contrast, you are unlikely to see any male bisexual activity at the Candy Store. There are men who like that on occasion, but if they do it at the Candy Store, they go to a private room together. There are some men who are so homophobic that in a foursome situation they get nervous if any part of their body comes into contact with another man. Others have no trouble with the contact that is virtually inevitable in an MFM threesome, even though there is no bisexual activity.

So what would you see if you wandered around at the Candy Store? You would see lots of enticing glimpses of public nudity here and there. You would see many couples having sex, some married to each other and most not. You would see MFM and FMF threesomes going on. You would see same room foursomes, same bed foursomes, and full swap couples. You would see one woman enjoying three men at once. You would see men and women who meet in the hot tub get acquainted and then flow into each other's arms. Nearly always this is in the context of sex as play in the best sense of the term.

You would see people of diverse cultures overcome hesitations and enjoy a meeting of the bodies. You would see men put aside their qualms and kiss their wives while their wives' mouths are still hot from vigorously sucking other men. In so doing they lift up and affirm their wives and strengthen their marriage.

Any sane person reading this would be wondering about disease. I have asked many members who have been coming to (and at) the Candy Store for years. Not one can remember hearing of a single sexually transmitted infection at the Candy Store. There's plenty of gossip at the Candy Store, and I assume that sort of thing would get around among these people. What they agree is very common, though, is the sharing of colds. I suppose this is an occupational hazard. (It may be that the low prevalence of STIs is because those at the Candy Store are generally married, mid-thirties or older, and often play only with other Candy Store members. It's an almost closed circle. I've talked with several women who have contracted genital herpes, but not in a club.)

Many men wear condoms, and some women insist on it. Because there is so much playing available, if a man would rather not wear a condom, a couple can choose to not play together with no hard feelings. Some men will say, "I don't want to use a condom because it makes my erection wilt, so how about if I just eat you?" Who would say no to that? (By the way, if you refuse to give oral sex to women, just stay away. Refusing to satisfy a woman that way is not polite at a swing club.) There may be a few women using dental dams for oral sex, but it's rare. Anal sex seems to be unusual at the Candy Store, though it's possible that it happens behind closed doors.

There are clubs of "beautiful people" in Los Angeles and Miami where people stand around exchanging the names of their plastic surgeons and showing off their latest boob jobs, tummy tucks, and face lifts. There are people at the Candy Store who have had surgery—primarily breast augmentation—and if so there are a few jokes, admiring glances and touches, and congratulations, but it's not common.

By contrast, at the Candy Store people notice when their friends have lost twenty pounds or more—or put it on. The Candy Store is paradise for those who love sex, but doubly so for larger people who love sex. Because nearly everyone is well beyond the government weight recommendations, yet sexually interested, nearly everyone is also sexually interesting.

There are many dance clubs where larger people are ignored or even taunted. At the Candy Store they find full acceptance. Certainly some are more attractive than others, and some get more offers than others, but at the Candy Store both men and women know that the ability to give and receive pleasure is only partially restricted by weight. It is wonderful for heavier people to receive ardent attention. It does wonders for their self-confidence. It's no wonder that many Candy Store members who aren't married choose to only have relationships at the club. The physical couplings may be brief, but it is easy to develop friendships that are comfortably maintained over years. It's a bit like the bar where *Friends* is set, but with "benefits." For many people, a friendly and only occasionally sexual relationship is much more satisfying than the demands of marriage.

The group that has the roughest time at the Candy Store is single men. Some are voyeurs who do not want any physical relationship but merely want to watch. Some, perhaps, are exhibitionists who want to expose themselves. Neither is a problem at the Candy Store, though voyeurs and exhibitionists are considered a bit pathetic and avoided or ignored. Some, whatever their age, have a pleasantness and self-confidence that help them make acquaintances and then friends. These men have little trouble finding partners.

The ones who have trouble, irrespective of age and looks, are the ones who are too shy to say hello to people or ask women to dance. These men stand at the edges, gazing longingly. Some women turn away from them with disgust. Others feel sorry for them. But they don't usually feel sorry enough to play. Other men may understand what they are going through, yet hesitate to give them pointers that might dilute the pool of available women. They feel bad about these men paying $90 and going away unhappy, but sex is not for sale at the Candy Store, and there is no guarantee of success.

Clubs like the Candy Store are not rare, but there are a lot of variations one might find. Some clubs are fancier, with nicer hot tubs, more attractive decoration, and better food. Some clubs are more rudimentary, with no hot tub, no food or only some light snacks, few private rooms, or no specialty rooms (these are usually cheaper). Some face ordinances that allow vinyl-covered and padded platforms but not mattresses and sheets. Some clubs have liquor licenses. Some clubs are in cities, though they may be in warehouse or strip club districts. Most clubs require memberships and have yearly fees as well as nightly fees, but some don't require advance registration.

Apart from some of the single guys, everyone at the Candy Store seems to win. In the entire world of sex, the sort of swing club represented by the Candy Store seems to be nearly as close to paradise as sex lovers can get in their lifetimes if they want a lot of variety in one night. The sex is free, willing, guiltless, and, with proper precautions, less high risk than at singles' bars. The relationships are very healthy, with little jealousy or violence. The emphasis on playing rather than on orgasms is liberating. People who visit the Candy Store regularly comment that the world would be a much nicer and safer place if everyone went someplace like the Candy Store every weekend. They are probably right.

At the Candy Store, as at most swing clubs, the number one rule is "No means no!" If a man follows a woman around watching her or trying to get her to play with him when she has said no or told him to get lost, he will be thrown out of the club within minutes of when she complains to an attendant, and he'll never be allowed back in. Rape is pretty well impossible because every other man in the club will protect any woman who cries out for help. It's always women who decide who they want to play with. There may be occasions when a woman has sex with a man who doesn't interest her so her partner can have sex with that man's partner, but men do the same just as often. More commonly, couples have their own rules, such as "We only play with a couple if we both want to—no complaints or hard feelings."

Still, it's likely that the majority of sex seekers would not feel comfortable at a swing club. We all have ideas of right and wrong, and even AFF members may not be ready to freely exchange partners or have several partners in a night or at a time.

Also, it's very common for people who have been to clubs and loved them, whether occasionally or frequently, to lose interest. Sometimes this is because of a bad experience (say, being told that one is too old or too heavy or too small). Sometimes people simply lose interest. One woman told me, "My husband and I have been doing this for twenty-five years, but our hearts just aren't in it anymore, so we've decided to leave the swing lifestyle, at least for awhile." People who have been wildly excited at clubs may come to feel that there's no one they really want to play with. The thrill is gone. Many decide that they'd like to return to sexual exclusivity. Even paradise can grow stale.

Meanwhile, what does swinging like this do for marriages? Very little scholarly research has been published on swinging in the past quarter century. Arline M. Rubin and James R. Adam wrote, in their

1986 article "Outcomes of Sexually Open Marriages," "This study follows up a 1978 matched
sample of 82 couples to find out if there were differences in marital stability between the sexually
open and the sexually exclusive couples. In 1983 no
statistically significant difference in marital stability was found. Of couples providing follow-up
data, 23 (68%) of the 34 sexually open couples and
32 (82%) of the 39 sexually exclusive couples were
still together. . . .

"On the question, specifically, of the effect of
the sexual openness on the stability of the marriages, we have found no reliable evidence of differences between the two groups. The reasons
given for marital breakup were almost never related to extramarital sex.

"Are outcomes of sexually open marriages different from sexually exclusive marriages? We
found no generalized differences, for better or
for worse."

In 2008 doctoral dissertation on this topic,
Edward Fernandes found that swingers were more
satisfied with their spouses than are married couples in the general population.

In many ways, going to swing clubs is a lot more
satisfying than trying to develop online sexual relationships. If you find someone on AFF who you like
a lot and who likes a lot of sex, perhaps you should

share this chapter and suggest a road trip to a swing club.

For lists of swing clubs, find the web sites of NASCA or SwingLifeStyle. You may need to join to get access to the lists. The lists will send you to the web sites of the clubs.

Chapter 3:
Having Fun at Swinging House Parties

Most people—even people on AdultFriend-Finder—have never even heard of house parties, and I know of no scholarly account of one. If you have already experienced and loved house parties, this chapter won't teach you much, but will simply confirm what you already know. If you haven't been to a house party or have tried one but had a bad experience, this chapter may whet your appetite or help you understand why the party you went to wasn't what you'd expected.

Many sex lovers prefer to share themselves with only one other person or couple in an evening, and lots don't even go that far, preferring to develop long-term friendships with only one person or couple besides their significant other. However, for those who love having a variety of partners in one night, there is an option that is sometimes even better than swing clubs at their best: house parties. A house party might be defined as a group of people who gather for friendship, food, flirting, and, most importantly, sex in a private home. If a swing club can be paradise, a good house party must be beyond paradise—heaven itself with a choir of angels. (Hotel suite parties are similar: perhaps five to ten couples meeting together in a suite or hotel room. In this chapter we can lump them together, as they have similar dynamics.)

Not all house parties, of course, are good ones from the point of view of those who crave lots of sex with lots of people. For these people, what would constitute a failed house party? If there's no swinging going on, it's not a swinger's party—at most it's a cocktail party or a friendly get-together where people talk about sex. One couple in their sixties told me, "We went to a house party expecting that everyone would be playing. Instead, no one played at all. The women sat around the dining room eating the food and talking about their kids and sex. The men stood in the kitchen talking about sports and sex. But there was no sex." Another couple told me, "We sometimes go to house parties where most people seem to want to watch, and only a few want to be watched." There are also house parties where you might feel very ill at ease because the other people don't seem to be "your sort of people," whatever your sort might be.

Factors That Help Make a Party a Success

Do you want to throw a house party? Do you want to be able to foresee which parties are likely to be really hot? There seem to be several things that help make a house party a success. One is critical mass. Whether at clubs or house parties, it sometimes seems that there needs to be a certain density per cubic yard before things get interesting. Parties may seem dull at first, but when enough people are there, they become more lively.

Also, the time can influence the level of action. Sometimes a party that seems dull at eight or ten picks up suddenly around eleven. Some couples leave around midnight or one, yet it seems that there is often a surge of activity around two before people bunk down somewhere.

Another factor is homogeneity of age, class, taste, and looks. People are most comfortable playing with people like themselves. If a twentysomething couple comes to a party where everyone else is in their forties, the younger couple may think the older people ugly or even elderly. (This sometimes comes as a shock to those of us who are older, but if we recall how people our present age looked to us a few decades back, we may admit that we would have felt the same.) Meanwhile, the older couples may think the younger couples are too young to know much about being good lovers (and that may be true). Age variety is acceptable if people are used to it, but if they aren't, it can slow down a party.

We all know that at any age, some people are better looking than other people. Some people are in excellent physical condition, whatever their age, and some aren't. Some are what we call height/weight proportionate, and some aren't. Some people tolerate obese people, and others prefer partners who are obese. Some people accept a wide variety of ages and looks, while others will only play with those they consider very attractive. Parties seem to work better if there is some homogeneity of looks, if most of the people there are similar in looks or tolerate people with those looks.

It isn't always easy to know if you will like what you find at a party. Sometimes it's what we might call "pot-luck." Some hosts send out a list of the names of those attending, or their handles on SLS, AFF, or APG (AltPlayGround). This is nice, as it can whet people's appetites. It also allows people to quietly cancel if it looks like few of those signed up are their kind of people. Sometimes people enter a home, are introduced to people, and secretly think, "There's no one here I want to play with." Still, if they stay around and chat, they often discover that there are several people who become quite attractive as the evening progresses.

Many people are uncomfortable talking about social class or even deny that it exists. But it does exist. There are several types of social class in America. One is based on income. People of similar income levels may have that at least in common, yet they might differ in other ways. Another type of social class is based on education and employment. People with graduate degrees often get along well with other people with graduate degrees. Computer specialists often get along well with other computer specialists. Mechanics often get along well with other mechanics. People in business know how to talk to other people in business. Yet another type of class is based on privilege, the right schools, clubs, and neighborhoods.

Different classes often have different tastes. For example, in some classes, a man thinks himself handsome in a baseball cap. In another class, a man in a baseball cap is scorned. In some classes, boots or camouflage are considered attractive. In other classes, they are not. In some classes, tattoos on men and women are almost expected and are considered attractive. In some classes, piercings are considered worthy of admiration. In other classes, they are embarrassing. In some classes, trucks are the vehicles of choice, but not in all classes. I mention this not to put down one group or another, but to point out that not everyone is comfortable with every option. Parties tend to work best when people have similar tastes, whatever their incomes.

An attractive middle-aged couple proud of their tattoos and piercings may intimidate attractive middle-aged couples who aren't used to them or don't like them. In turn, they may notice that they are intimidating and feel uncomfortable. Likewise, a couple without tattoos and piercings may feel very out of place at a house party where most people have them.

Class and taste also includes housing. Most people are comfortable visiting people who live in houses like their own. Often they are uncomfortable visiting houses they consider significantly below or above their own in size or quality. It can be embarrassing when someone who lives in a small but comfortable lower middle class home goes to a party in a large, beautiful home and is obviously abashed or starts asking the price of everything. Similarly, those who live in the larger home may feel quite uncomfortable in the smaller home. Also, people of different classes are sometimes comfortable with different levels of cleanliness and neatness. One couple told me, "We went to a house party where the kitchen was so filthy and cluttered that there was no place to put down any-thing, and we felt like we were about to catch some disease." Other people were having fun, but they weren't, so they left. On the other hand, their own house was filled with crafts, knick-knacks, and photos of children and grandchildren, and some might be uncomfortable in that sort of home.

Taste includes taste in music, art, books, mov-ies, and television. It includes taste in furnishings, clothing, vehicles, amusement, and exercise. I men-tion this not to claim that one taste is better than another, but to assert that often house parties go best when there is some general homogeneity of taste. Further, when people at a house party dis-cover that they like the same books, programs, mu-sic, or furniture, they are well on their way to en-joying themselves and perhaps building a bond that will lead to future meetings.

Homogeneity is not required, but it does help house parties succeed. There is plenty of room for variation within limits, but large variations can be challenging or even ruin a party. One exception is when individuals are invited who are quite differ-ent, but are able to prove themselves likeable and themselves like the other people present. A few people like this can add spice to a house party and also help people become more tolerant of varia-tions.

This is sometimes the case with various ethnic groups. Some people are comfortable with a house party where a variety of ethnicities are represented. More, though, prefer a house party where only their own ethnicity is found or where only a small number of people of other ethnicities is found. For example, African-Americans who throw house parties know that there are some whites who are very comfortable with them or even prefer them, but others who would be wildly uncomfortable in a party with only a few whites. Those same uncomfortable whites might be very comfortable when there are only one or two African-American couples at a house party, and they may even enjoy playing with them. Of course, the right people of other ethnicities to invite to your party are the ones who are comfortable and can face a bit of prejudice without taking offence. A black man at a large party where nearly everyone is white can have a very good time indeed, especially if he is polite, well-spoken, and doesn't have a chip on his shoulder. If he is tempted to feel hurt if he is rejected by some women, he should bear in mind that those same women are probably rejecting most of the other men, too.

Another factor in success is matching play interests. If one woman invited is bisexual, it's nice if several are. If you expect male bisexual action at your party, many men will want to know in advance, as this is less common and less acceptable to some than bisexual female activities. Some people enjoy a touch of bondage, but some don't. Some love to dress like, act like, or actually be doms or dommes, masters or mistresses, but others find bondage repellent. Some men enjoy wearing nylons and garter belts, panties and bras, but most men seem to find that intimidating (especially if it is middle-aged men in drag). There is a wide variety of fetishes. Most of these are best practiced in groups of people who enjoy them, not at the average house party. The idea is to have people who are similar enough to enjoy each other. It's rare that everyone is interested in everyone, but at the least it's nice if any couple you invite can find three or four other couples who seem compatible. The more compatible people are, the more fun they will have.

Getting the Party Started

In addition to critical mass, time, and homogeneity, it helps to have some "party starters" on hand. When people have arrived, eaten a few snacks, and had a drink or two, a sexual tension often begins to build. People have eyed each other, chatted with each other, and tried to get a sense of who might be interested and available, yet no one has the nerve to make the first move. This might continue for another hour or two—wasting half the evening—or the ice might be broken by some brave person or couple. Such people should be recognized and prized. Perhaps they simply stand in the center of the living room and begin undressing. Perhaps, disrobed, they begin moving from person to person, inviting fondling or tasting. If they do this, usually the party comes to life within minutes. Perhaps they each choose a partner, pull the person to his or her feet, and begin undressing the person, or perhaps they lead the person to a bed.

Some house party hosts assume that hosting the party is enough, but there are also many icebreakers hosts can use to get people going. There are of course such ancient children's games as spin-the-bottle or strip poker or various games involving dares. There are newer card games that ask people to do various sexy things. These are good for titillation, but they can also waste an hour that might be better devoted to other fun. Fashion shows of sexy lingerie sometimes work, and they have the added benefit of getting people out of their street clothes. One host couple made it clear in their invitations that everyone was expected to be at the party by 8:30 and nude or in party attire by 9:00. To add to the fun, they filled the living room floor with eight or ten mattresses, announced that this was to be an "oral and toys only" hour, and set a timer that went off every fifteen minutes, at which time everyone had to change partners. By the end of the hour, even those who knew no one else when they arrived knew at least certain parts of four other people quite intimately.

At another party, the hostess chose three couples, announced that they must strip, blindfolded the men and had them lie on the living room floor, then shuffled the women and instructed each to fellate the man in front of her. Every couple minutes the women changed partners until each had sucked each man. Then the men had to write down the order in which the women had sucked them. Could they identify their own partners? Then the women were blindfolded, and the men had their own oral opportunities. The women were much better at guessing the men than the men were at guessing the women. By the time this exhibition was completed, everyone was ready for fun.

Many hosts see showing x-rated movies on television as a good ice breaker. Perhaps it is at times. The problem is that sometimes people sit around watching videos rather than acting them out. Some people would rather watch than play, yes, but if you are hosting your own house party, that may not be the sort of people you want to invite. Those who are a bit shy need the encouragement of being dragged to a mattress, not the sight of sex on the screen. Where x-rated movies may be more useful is after people are already playing. Then, when people take a break, a movie may help them focus on why they are at the party and help them gain the stamina to return to the fray.

House Parties vs. Clubs

Some readers who have enjoyed clubs may think there can be nothing better. How does a club differ from a house party? Well, it's usually cheaper to attend a house party. Some are free, while some charge between $5 and $25 to cover the cost of food and drink. Many hosts ask people to bring their own bottles. Often people are asked to bring some snacks. By comparison, many couples pay $75 or more to attend a club, plus the beverages they bring, and single men often pay $100 or more. Then there is often the cost of a motel room or an extra charge to stay overnight at the club.

People who go to clubs may know very few of the people there unless they go to that club often and it has a very faithful clientele. Clubs often depend on disk jockeys, a good dance floor, loud music, and flashing lights to get people up and dancing, and the dance floor is perhaps the best place to meet new people at a club. Many people go to clubs merely to drink and dance. They like the sexy dancing and loose conversation, but they don't want to play. Dancing sometimes happens at large house parties, but it's less important, and it's primarily an ice breaker. Sometimes the ice doesn't break unless quite a few people are dancing. Thus, if it's dancing you want, it's generally better to go to a club.

If what you want is a variety of partners, a good house party is generally the best choice. Quite a few partygoers report that they generally have five to eight partners in an evening, whereas they may have two to five at a club. Some are much pickier or much less fortunate, of course. However, it seems fair to say that those who do very well for themselves at a club do even better at a house party.

In general, the group dynamic at house parties or hotel suite parties is quite different from the group dynamic at clubs. At clubs, a lot of the women are there to be seen and admired. Many women change their costume two or three times in an evening, not because the costume is dirty, but because they enjoy showing off. The dynamic at a swing club is different from that at a dance club or a singles bar, as mentioned in the previous chapter. Still, while there is less of the "meat market" feel at a swing club, given that most people admit to themselves and to others that they are there to play, there is quite a bit of seduction going on. Admittedly, the seduction is easier. Still, men have to get up their nerve to talk to women, invite them to dance. Or women must ask the men. With every dance, partners are sizing each other up, chatting perhaps, trying to figure out if the other person is interested. At a club, there might be two hundred people, yet the majority of those people might ignore you, look right past you. There might be a lot of people you are willing to play with and a few you would try to seduce. Meanwhile, it may be that a few people are hoping to seduce you, but you may never find out. At a club, a lot of people who want to play may not get the opportunity because they are shy or their looks are wrong for that crowd.

At a house party, it is usually much easier to get partners. People may see other people they hope to play with, but because there are usually relatively few people there and because the music is generally low enough so people can hear each other and because people are often standing around chatting or sitting around a living room or sitting in a hot tub, it's much easier to join a group and join the conversation. At a club, there are often cliques. People sometimes only talk with, dance with, or play with the people they came with. That's unusual behavior at a house party. There are many house parties where most people know and like each other, but if newcomers are invited, they are invited so they can be played with, so excluding them makes no sense. There are other house parties where few of the people know each other, but again, when the group is relatively small, it's harder to leave people out.

At clubs it's easier for single women to find partners than for single men, but even so it sometimes takes some courage and initiative. The fate of men at clubs is very sad unless they are good-looking and self-confident or unless they came only to watch. A large percentage of men who come alone don't get to play. The ideal commodity at swing clubs is women, and single men don't have any to trade, so couples are less likely to invite them to a room.

Single women at house parties can't easily hide, and the relaxed nature of smaller parties lends itself to female conversation. There is also a lot more support, both from other women and from men. Once single women get started playing at a house party, they can usually easily find partners until they are no longer interested. Single men also do better at house parties. It's easier for them to get into conversations with both groups of men and groups of women, as well as mixed groups. Once they are part of the conversation, they become known quantities and no longer outsiders. It may take a bit of courage to get started, but if everyone is naked and playing, a woman finished with one man often grabs for whomever is at hand. Once a single man is playing, it's easy to continue.

Men tend to wear out before women, and house parties are safe environments for women who want to be utterly satiated. Some hosts have discovered that it's good to invite a few single men to parties. For large parties, some actually invite some single men explicitly to serve as a second shift, arriving about eleven, when many men are petering out, but while the women are still avid. This is an ideal situation for a single man. However, the men who are asked back are the ones who are self-confident, likeable, well-hung, and very long-lasting. They are, after all, there to be studs. Does this sound degrading? Ask a stallion if he minds servicing lots of mares.

One important difference between clubs and house parties is how people react to older people. At clubs, most people in their thirties and forties find it pretty easy to find partners. People in their fifties find it a bit more difficult, particularly women. Most clubs have very few guests in their sixties or seventies. Those who do come may be treated politely, with women saying to their partners, "Oh, aren't they cute?" But there's an assumption that people their age should play with people their age, and there simply aren't many—or any. So they don't get to play.

By contrast, both men and women in their sixties and seventies who are in good health, good shape, and up for the action can easily find partners at house parties. This is especially the case if they go to house parties where they are known and loved. If a man of forty or fifty has played once with a woman of seventy and discovered how lovely she is, how talented she is, and how enjoyable she is, he is eager to play with her again, and she may be near the top of his list of favorites. If she is intelligent and interesting, so much the better. For many men, sex with an attractive woman in her seventies is an eye-opener. Whatever age we are, we tend to assume that people a generation older than we are can't function sexually. Once we have experienced the pleasure of older women, a new world is open to us—and a great many new potential partners are open to us, as well.

The same goes for men. In a house party setting, it's easier for older men to enter conversations and come to be seen as attractive by younger women. So long as they are potent—and in this day of Viagra, Cialis, and injections, it's much easier to be potent—they can perform. Those who are impotent can at least use their tongues and hands so long as they are interested. One of the pleasures of age is realizing that providing pleasure for others can be as delightful as receiving pleasure.

In some house parties, the hosts remove the bright lights, substituting dimmer, more flattering lights. Add to this the fact that many people remove glasses or contacts before playing. The result is that men and woman both may look much younger than they really are. A woman of fifty-five may look thirty-five to her lover, and what woman wouldn't love to be honestly seen by her partner as twenty years younger than she really is?

The Special Dynamic of House Party Sex

The dynamic of the first hour or two of a house party is very different from both the beginning of an evening at a club and from a first meeting with a person or couple at a restaurant or bar. However, what for many sex lovers makes house parties better than paradise is the dynamic during the playing.

Many people at house parties prefer to play in private rooms, but more are willing to play in groups or in open rooms than at swing clubs. Perhaps this is because more of the guests know each other or perhaps because it's easier to know each other.

It's in the open rooms that the special dynamic of house party sexuality is found. People are more relaxed, less self-conscious, more open to experimentation there than elsewhere. Imagine this. A woman is lying on her bed with her eyes closed, enjoying the feeling of a man pumping into her. Another man and a women kneel beside her and begin kissing her and sucking her breasts. The first man grows weary, but the second man takes his place while the two women kiss. Another man comes up and begins licking the second woman, then enters her. The second man finishes and begins kissing the second woman as the first woman slips away to wash. Now the second woman is the center of action. By various permutations, gradually the partners shift and various people become the center of attention. Playing may continue in that spot for several hours, with a dozen partners, yet no more than four at once. Meanwhile, a similar scene is going on at the other end of the bed and on the next bed over and in the room down the hall.

At its best, this dynamic is dreamlike. There is no need for alcohol or drugs. Those participating notice the many differences of looks, texture, odor, size, and technique, yet almost as if through a veil or in water. It's almost as if it were in slow motion. Partners slide in and out of the picture. There are no hard feelings, no arguments. There are cries of pleasure, grunts of passion. In a way, it's almost like a low-key, multi-hour orgasm. Some pull out for a break to clean up or grab something to drink or eat, then move to another bed and join another group already in progress. For those who love sexual variety, this is probably as good as it gets.

How do you get invited to a house party? It isn't easy. Some cities have groups of people who have been meeting together for years. Some of these are listed at APG or SLS. I know of one group with about three hundred members that has been meeting for around thirty years. Various members throw house parties—perhaps one a year, perhaps several. Because there are so many members, there is usually one or more every week. Usually the parties are limited to between ten and twenty-five couples. People sign up for parties hosted by their friends or by people with a reputation for good parties.

One good thing about being part of a group like this is that you hear about a lot of parties, and you can sign up for as many as you like. Another good thing is that you build a circle of acquaintances: people get to know you, your likes and dislikes, and your capabilities. Some couples who first meet at house parties end up getting together some other time for dinner or for playing or even go on vacations together. Some people enjoy the fact that by the time they've been to half a dozen parties thrown by group members, they recognize a large share of those present. Other people, however, grow weary of seeing the same people at party after party and would like more new faces.

If you visit a club or meet people online, you might try asking if they know of any groups of people who have house parties. If a couple knows that you play well with others, they may recommend you. There are thousands of special interest groups on AFF, and if you join local discussions, you can ask members if they know of anyone having house parties.

Not everyone is up to thoroughly enjoying house parties, just as not all sex lovers are interested in having more than one sexual partner at a time, but if you find the idea wildly exciting, try it.

Meanwhile, as with swing clubs, many sex lovers decide that they've had enough variety for the time being and stop going to house parties. Perhaps their interests change, or they have a bad experience, or they simply grow bored. Many go to parties for decades, but probably most do not. Priorities change. It doesn't matter, so long as the people remain happy with their lives.

This is a small book, but I hope you've learned a lot from it. We all know the old cliché, "Anything worth doing is worth doing well." People who spend a couple hours or days on AdultFriendFinder without success then give up have simply not put the effort into it that success requires. Do what I suggest and you will almost certainly succeed. Likewise, if you are a minute-man, you are not going to be very popular at a swing club or a house party, but with practice you can learn to stay hard for hours, and you can also learn to make yourself attractive to others in many ways. Don't give up. You can have fun online and offline, but practice always at getting good at it. Have fun.

Bibliography

Albright, Julie M. "Sex in America Online: An Exploration of Sex, Marital Status, and Sexual Identity in Internet Sex Seeking and Its Impacts." *Journal of Sex Research* 45.2 (2008): 175-186.

Allen, Ed, and Dana Allen. *Together Sex: The Playful Couple's Key to Enjoying Swinging.* N.p., MomentPoint, 1976.

Allen, Elizabeth S., & Donald H. Baucom. "Dating, Marital, and Hypothetical Extradyadic Involvements: How Do They Compare? *Journal of Sex Research* 43.4 (2006): 307-317.

Allen, Elizabeth S., and Galena K. Rhoades. "Not All Affairs Are Created Equal: Emotional Involvement with an Extradyadic Partner." *Journal of Sex & Marital Therapy* 34 (2008): 51-65.

Allen, Elizabeth S., Galena Kline Rhoades, Scott M. Stanley, Howard J. Markman, Tamara Williams, Jessica Melton, and Mari L. Clements. "Premarital Precursors of Marital Infidelity." *Family Process* 47.2 (2008): 243-259.

Anapol, Deborah M. *Polyamory: The New Love Without Limits: Secrets of Sustainable Intimate Relationships.* San Rafael: Inti-Net, 1997.

Anderlini-D'Onofrio, Serena, ed. *Plural Loves: Designs for Bi and Poly Living* New York: Routledge, 2005.

Barash, David P., and Judith Eve Lipton. *The Myth of Monogamy: Fidelity and Infidelity in Animals and People.* New York: W. H. Freeman, 2001.

Bernard, J., "Infidelity: Some Moral and Social Issues." In J. R. Smith and L. G. Smith, ed., *Beyond Monogamy* (Baltimore: Johns Hopkins UP, 1974).

Bartell, Gilbert D. *Group Sex: A Scientist's Eyewitness Report on the American Way of Swinging.* New York: Wyden, 1971.

Baumeister, Roy F., Kathleen R. Catanese, & Kathleen D. Vohs. "Is There a Gender Difference in Strength of Sex Drive? Theoretical Views, Conceptual Distinctions, and a Review of Relevant Evidence." *Personality and Social Psychology Review* 5.3 (2001): 242–273.

Beach, Steven R. H., Ernest N. Jouriles, & D. K. O'Leary. (1985). "Extramarital Sex: Impact on Depression and Commitment in Couples Seeking Marital Therapy." *Journal of Sex & Marital Therapy* 11 (1985), 99–108.

Becker, Vaughn D., Brad J. Sagarin, Rosanna E. Guadagno, Allison Millevoi, Lionel D. Nicastle. "When the Sexes Need Not Differ: Emotional Responses to the Sexual and Emotional Aspects of Infidelity." *Personal Relationships* 11.4 (2004): 529-538.

Bellemeade, Kaye. *Swinging for Beginners: An Introduction to the Lifestyle*. N.p.: New Tradition, 2003.

Bergstrand, Curtis, and Jennifer Blevins Williams. "Today's Alternative Marriage Styles: The Case of Swingers." *Electronic Journal of Human Sexuality* 3 (October 10, 2000). 30 March 2009 <http://www.ejhs.org/volume3/swing/body.htm>.

Berman, Laura. *Real Sex for Real Women*. London: DK Adult, 2008.

Berman, Laura, Jennifer Berman, and Alice Burdick Schweiger. *Secrets of the Sexually Satisfied Woman: Ten Keys to Unlocking Ultimate Pleasure*. New York: Hyperion, 2005.

Blow, Adrian J., & Kelley Hartnett. "Infidelity in Committed Relationships I: A Methodological Review. *Journal of Marital and Family Therapy* 31.2 (2005): 183-216.

Blow, Adrian J., & Kelley Hartnett. "Infidelity in Committed Relationships II: A Substantive Review. *Journal of Marital and Family Therapy* 31.2 (2005): 217-233.

Boekhout, Brock A., Susan S. Hendrick, and Clyde Hendrick. "Exploring Infidelity: Developing the Relationship Issues Scale." *Journal of Loss and Trauma* 8.4 (2003): 283-306.

Bogle, Kathleen. *Hooking Up: Sex, Dating, and Relationships on Campus*. New York: New York UP, 2008.

Brandt, Judith. *The 50-Mile Rule: Your Guide to Infidelity and Extramarital Etiquette*. Berkeley: Ten Speed Press, 2002.

Breedlove, William. *Swap Clubs: A Study in Contemporary Sexual Mores*. Los Angeles: Sherbourne, 1964.

Brown, Jane D. "Mass Media Influences on Sexuality." *Journal of*

Sex Research 39.1 (2002): 42-45.

Brown, Julia S. "A Comparative Study of Deviation from Sexual Mores." *American Sociological Review* 17.2 (1952): 135-146.

Buss, David M. *The Evolution of Desire: Strategies of Human Mating*, rev. New York: Basic, 2003.

Buunk, Bram P. "Sex, Self-Esteem, Dependency and Extradyadic Sexual Experience as Related to Jealousy Responses." *Journal of Social and Personal Relationships* 12.1 (1995): 147-153.

Buxton, Amity Pierce. "Writing Our Own Script: How Bisexual Men and Their Heterosexual Wives Maintain Their Marriages After Disclosure." *Journal of Bisexuality* 4.2/3 (2001): 155-190. 10.1 (1974): 21-31.

Byers, E. Sandra. "Relationship Satisfaction and Sexual Satisfaction: A Longitudinal Study of Individuals in Long-Term Relationships. *Journal of Sex Research* 42.2 (2005): 113–118.

Call, Vaughn, Susan Sprecher, and Pepper Schwartz. "The Incidence and Frequency of Marital Sex in a National Sample." *Journal of Marriage and the Family* 57.3 (1995): 639–652.

Charny, Israel W., and Sivan Parnass. "The Impact of Extramarital Relationships on the Continuation of Marriages." *Journal of Sex & Marital Therapy* 21.2 (1995): 100-115.

Chernus, Linda A. "Sexual Mate-Swapping: A Comparison of 'Normal' and 'Clinical' Populations." *Clinical Social Work Journal* 8.2 (1980): 120-130.

Choi, Kyung-hee, Joseph A. Catania, and M. Margaret Dolcini. "Extramarital Sex and HIV Risk Behavior among US Adults: Results from the National AIDS Behavioral Survey." *American Journal of Public Health* 84.12 (1994): 2003-2007.

Colson, Marie-Hélène, Antoine Lemaire, Philippe Pinton, Karim Hamidi, and Patrick Klein. "Sexual Behaviors and Mental Perception, Satisfaction and Expectations of Sex Life in Men and Women in France. *Journal of Sexual Medicine* 3.1 ((2006): 121–131.

Constantine, Larry L., and Joan M. Constantine. *Group Marriage: A Study of Contemporary Multilateral Marriage*. New York: Collier, 1974.

Cooper, Al. *Cybersex: The Dark Side of the Force: A Special Issue of the Journal Sexual Addiction and Compulsion*. New York: Routledge, 2000.

Cooper, Al, David L. Delmonico, and Ron Burg. "Cybersex Users, Abusers, and Compulsives: New Findings and Implications. *Sexual Addictions & Compulsivity* 7 (2000): 5-29.

Cooper, Alvin, Coralie R. Scherer, Sylvain C. Boies, and Barry L. Gordon. "Sexuality on the Internet: From Sexual Exploration to Pathological Expression." *Professional Psychology: Research & Practice* 30.2 (1999): 154-164.

Davidson, Joy. "Working With Polyamorous Clients In The Clinical Setting." *Electronic Journal of Human Sexuality* 5 (April 16, 2002). 31 March 2009 <http://www.ejhs.org/volume5/polyoutline.html>.

Denfield, Duane. "Dropouts from Swinging." *Family Coordinator* 23.1 (1974): 45-49.

Denfield, Duane, and Michael Gordon. "The Sociology of Mate Swapping: Or the Family that Swings Together Clings Together." *Journal of Sex Research* 6.2 (1970): 85-100.

DeSalvo, Louise. *Adultery*. Boston: Beacon, 2000.

de Visser, Richard. "Swings and roundabouts: Management of Jealousy in Heterosexual 'Swinging' Couples." *British Journal of Social Psychology* 46.2 (2007): 459-476.

Easton, Dossie, and Catherine A. Lizst. *The Ethical Slut: A Guide to Infinite Sexual Possibilities*. San Francisco: Greenery, 1997.

Elliot, Leland, and Cynthia Brantley. *Sex on Campus: The Details Guide to the Real Sex Lives of College Students*. Princeton: Princeton Review, 1997.

Emens, Elizabeth F. "Monogamy's Law: Compulsory Monogamy and Polyamorous Existence." *New York University Review of Law and Social Change* 29 (2004): 277-376. 30 Mar. 2009 <http://www.lexisnexis.com:80/us/lnacademic/results/docview/docview.do?risb=21_T6180148924&treeMax=false&sort=&docNo=1&format=GNBFI&startDocNo=0&treeWidth=0&nodeDisplayName=&cisb=&reloadPage=false>.

Fang, Betty. "Swinging in Retrospect." *Journal of Sex Research* 12.3 (1976): 220-238.

Fernandes, Edward M. *The Swinging Paradigm: An Evaluation of the Marital and Sexual Satisfaction of Swingers*. Diss. Union Institute and University, Cincinnati, Ohio, 2008. 30 Mar. 2009 < http://www.ejhs.org/Volume12/Swinging.htm>.

Ferree, Marnie C. "Women and the Web: Cybersex Activity and Implications." *Sexual and Relationship Therapy* 18.3 (2003): 385-393.

Fisher, Helen. *Anatomy of Love: A Natural History of Mating, Marriage, and Why We Stray.* New York: Ballentine, 1994.

Fisher, Helen. *Why We Love: The Nature and Chemistry of Romantic Love.* New York: Henry Holt, 2004.

Garcia, Luis T., and Charlotte Markey. Matching in Sexual Experience for Married, Cohabitating, and Dating Couples. *Journal of Sex Research* 44.3 (2007): 250-255.

Glass, Shirley P., and Thomas L. Wright. "The Relationship of Extramarital Sex, Length of Marriage, and Sex Differences on Marital Satisfaction and Romanticism: Athanasiou's Data Reanalyzed." *Journal of Marriage & Family* 39.4 (1977): 691-703.

Glass, Shirley P., and Thomas L. Wright. "Justifications for Extramarital Relationships: The Association between Attitudes, Behaviors, and Gender." *Journal of Sex Research* 29.3 (1992): 361–387.

Goss, Robert E. "Proleptic Sexual Love: God's Promiscuity Reflected in Christian Polyamory." *Theology & Sexuality: Journal of the Institute for the Study of Christianity & Sexuality* 11.1 (2004): 52-63.

Gould, Terry. *The Lifestyle: A Look at the Erotic Rites of Swingers.* Tonawanda: Firefly, 2000.

Hart, Jon. [History of Plato's Retreat.] In Russ Kick's *Everything You Know About Sex Is Wrong: The Disinformation Guide to the Extremes of Human Sexuality (and Everything In Between).* New York: Disinformation Company, 2005.

Hertlein, Katherine M., Rose Ray, Joseph L. Wetchler, and J. Mark Killmer. "The Role of Differentiation in Extradyadic Relationships." *Journal of Couple & Relationship Therapy* 2.4 (2003): 33-50.

Hicks, Thomas V., and Harold Leitenberg. "Sexual Fantasies About One's Partner Versus Someone Else: Gender Differences in Incidence and Frequency." *Journal of Sex Research* 38/1 (2001): 43–50.

Hymer, S. M., & A. M. Rubin. "Alternative Lifestyle Clients: Therapists' Attitudes and Clinical Experiences. *Small Group Behavior* 13.4 (1982), 532-541. [Reported; not found.]

Ihara, Toni Lynne, Ralph E. Warner, and Frederick Hertz. *Living*

Together: A Legal Guide for Unmarried Couples, 13th ed. Berkeley: Nolo, 2006.

Janus, Samuel S., and Cynthia L. Janus. *The Janus Report on Sexual Behavior*. New York: Wiley, 1994.

Jenks, Richard J. "Swinging: A Replication and Test of a Theory." *Journal of Sex Research* 21.2 (1985): 199-206.

Jenks, Richard J. "Swinging: A Review of the Literature." *Archives of Sexual Behavior* 27.5 (1998): 507-521.

Johnson, Scott. "Your Cheatin' Heart: Myths and Absurdities About Extradyadic Relationships." *Journal of Couple & Relationship Therapy* 4.2/3 (2005): 161-172.

Juska, Jane. *A Round-Heeled Woman: My Late-Life Adventures in Sex and Romance*. New York: Villard, 2003.

Kenrick, Douglas T., Sara E. Gutierres, and Laurie L. Goldberg. "Influence of Popular Erotica on Judgments of Strangers and Mates," *Journal of Experimental Social Psychology* 25.2 (1989): 159–167.

Knapp, Jacquelyn J. Some Non-monogamous Marriage Styles and Related Attitudes and Practices of Marriage Counselors. *The Family Coordinator* 24.4 (1975), 505-514.

Kurdek, Lawrence A., and J. Patrick Schmitt. "Relationship Quality of Gay Men in Closes or Open Relationships." *Journal of Homosexuality* 12.2 (1985/1986): 85-99.

Lance, L. M. "Gender Differences in Heterosexual Dating: A Content Analysis of Personal Ads." *Journal of Men's Studies* 6 (1998): 297–305.

LaSala, Michael C. "Monogamy of the Heart: Extradyadic Sex and Gay Male Couples." *Journal of Gay and Lesbian Social Services* 17.3 (2004): 1-24.

Laumann, Edward O., John H. Gagnon, Robert T. Michael, and Stuart Michaels. *The Social Organization of Sexuality: Sexual Practices in the United States*. Chicago: U of Chicago P, 2000.

Lawson, Annette. *Adultery: An Analysis of Love and Betrayal*. New York: Basic, 1988.

Leitenberg, Harold, Mark J. Detzer, and Debra Srebnik. (1993). "Gender Differences in Masturbation and the Relation of Masturbation Experience in Preadolescence and/or Early Adolescence to Sexual Behavior and Sexual Adjustment in Young Adulthood." *Archives of Sexual Behavior* 22.2 (1993): 87-98.

Lister, Ashley. *Swingers: True Confessions from Today's Swinging Scene*. London: Virgin, 2006.

Macklin, Eleanor D. "Education for Choice: Implications of Alternatives in Lifestyles for Family Life Education." *Family Relations* 30.4 (1981): 567-577.

Mason, Michael. *The Making of Victorian Sexuality*. Oxford: Oxford UP, 1995.

Mazur, Ronald. The New Intimacy: Open-Ended Marriage and Alternative Lifestyles. Bloomington: iUniverse, 2000.

Miller, S. Andrea, & Elizabeth S. Byers. "Actual and Desired Duration of Foreplay and Intercourse: Discordance and Misperceptions within Heterosexual Couples." *Journal of Sex Research*, 41.3 (2004): 301-309.

Mint, Pepper. "The Power Dynamics of Cheating: Effects on Polyamory and Bisexuality." *Journal of Bisexuality* 4.3/4 (2004): 55-76.

Moore, Jerry L. *A Private Diary: Our First Year in Swinging*. West Conshohocken: Infinity, 2005.

Morell, Virginia. "A New Look at Monogamy." *Science* 281 (25 September 1998): 1982-1983.

Munson, Marcia, and Judith P. Steboum. "Introduction: The Lesbian Polyamory Reader: Open Relationships, Non-Monogamy, and Casual Sex." *Journal of Lesbian Studies* 3.1/2 (1999): 1-7.

Peabody, Shelley Anne. "Alternative Life Styles to Monogamous Marriage: Variants of Normal Behavior in Psychotherapy Clients." *Family Relations* 31.3 (1982): 425-434.

Perel, Esther. *Mating in Captivity: Reconciling the Erotic and the Domestic*. San Francisco: HarperCollins, 2006.

Phillis, Diane E., and Mark H. Gromko. (1985). "Gender Differences in Sexual Activity: Reality or Illusion." *Journal of Sex Research* 21.4 (1985): 437-448.

Pines, Ayala Malach. *Falling in Love: Why We Choose the Loves We Choose*, second ed. New York: Routledge, 2005.

Porter, Dawn. *Diaries of an Internet Lover*. London: Virgin, 2006.

Previti, Denise, and Paul R. Amato. "Is Infidelity a Cause or a Consequence of Poor Marital Quality?" *Journal of Social and Personal Relationship*, 21.2 (2004): 217-230.

Ramey, James W. "Intimate Groups and Networks: Frequent Consequence of Sexually Open Marriage." *Family Coordinator* 24.4

(1975): 515-530.

Ropelato, Jerry. "Internet Pornography Statistics"; 5 Feb. 2006 <http://internet-filter-review.toptenreviews.com/internet-por nography-statistics.html>

Rosenthal, Norman E. *The Emotional Revolution: How the New Science of Feelings Can Transform Your Life.* New York: Citadel, 2002.

Ross, Michael W. Typing, Doing, and Being: Sexuality and the Internet. *Journal of Sex Research* 42.4 (2005): 342-352.

Ross, Michael W., B. R. Simon Rosser, Sheryl McCurdy, and Jamie Feldman. "The Advantages and Limitations of Seeking Sex Online: A Comparison of Reasons Given for Online and Offline Sexual Liaisons by Men Who Have Sex with Men." *Journal of Sex Research* 44.1 (2007): 59-71.

Rowatt, Wade C., and David P. Schmitt. "Associations Between Religious Orientation and Varieties of Sexual Experience." *Journal for the Scientific Study of Religion* 42:3 (2003): 455-465.

Rubin, Arline M. "Sexually Open Versus Sexually Exclusive Marriage: A Comparison of Dyadic Adjustment." *Alternative Lifestyles* 5.2 (1982): 101-106.

Rubin, Arline M., & Adams, James R. (1986). "Outcomes of Sexually Open Marriages." *Journal of Sex Research* 22.3 (1986), 311-319.

Rubenstein, Herbert F., and Paul M. Margolis. *The Groupsex Tapes.* New York: McKay Company, 1971.

Santilla, Pekka, Ingrid Wager, Katarina Witting, Nicole Harlaar, Patrick Jern, Ada Johansson, Markus Varjonen, and N. Kenneth Sandnabba. "Discrepancies Between Sexual Desire and Sexual Activity: Gender Differences and Associations with Relationship Satisfaction." *Journal of Sex & Marital Therapy* 34 (2008): 31-44.

Sartorius, Annina. "Three and More in Love: Group Marriage or Integrating Commitment and Sexual Freedom." *Journal of Bisexuality* 4.3/4 (2004): 79-98.

Schmitt, David P., Todd K. Shackelford, and David M. Buss. "Are Men Really More 'Oriented' Toward Short-term Mating than Women?" *Psychology, Evolution & Gender* 3:3 (2001): 211-239.

Schmitt, David P. "The Big Five Related to Risky Sexual Behaviour Across 10 World Regions: Differential Personality Associations of Sexual Promiscuity and Relationship Infidelity." *European Journal of Personality* 18 (2004): 301-319.

Schmitt, David P., et al. "Universal Sex Differences in the Desire for Sexual Variety: Tests from 52 Nations, 6 Continents, and 13 Islands." *Journal of Personality and Social Psychology* 85.1 (2003): 85-104.

Schwartz, Pepper. *Everything You Know About Love and Sex Is Wrong.* New York: Perigee, 2001.

Schwartz, Pepper. *Prime: Adventures and Advice on Sex, Love, and the Sensual Years.* New York: Collins Living, 2007.

Seal, David Wyatt, Gina Agostinelli, and Charlotte A. Hannett. "Extradyadic Romantic Involvement: Moderating Effects of Sociosexuality and Gender." *Sex Roles* 31.1/2 (1994): 1-22.

Sheppard, Viveca J., Eileen S. Nelson, and Virginia Andreoli-Mathie. (1995). "Dating Relationships and Infidelity: Attitudes and Behaviors." *Journal of Sex & Marital Therapy* 21.3 (1995): 202-212.

Simbaxxx. *Doin One for the Team: Years in the Swinging Lifestyle.* North Charleston: BookSurge, 2006.

Smith, James R., and Lynn G. Smith, eds. *Beyond Monogamy: Recent Studies of Sexual Alternatives in Marriage.* Johns Hopkins UP, 1974.

Smith, Tom W. "The Sexual Revolution?" *Public Opinion Quarterly* 53.3 (1990): 415-435.

Spanier, Graham B., & Randie L. Margolis. (1983). "Marital Separation and Extramarital Sexual Behavior." *Journal of Sex Research* 19.1 (1983): 23-48.

"Statistics and Information on Pornography in the USA"; 5 Feb. 2006 <http://www.blazinggrace.org/pornstatistics.htm

Strassberg, Donald S., and Stephen Holty. "An Experimental Study of Women's Internet Personal Ads." *Archives of Sexual Behavior* 32.3 (2003): 253-260.

Thomas, Patti. *Recreational Sex: An Insider's Guide to the Swinging Lifestyle.* Cleveland: Peppermint, 2002.

Thompson, Anthony P. "Extramarital Sex: A Review of the Research Literature." *Journal of Sex Research* 19.1 (1983): 1-22.

Townsend, J. M., and G. D. Levy. "Effects of Partners' Physical Attractiveness and Socioeconomic Status on Sexuality and Partner Selection." *Archives of Sexual Behavior* 19 (1990): 149-164.

Updike, John. *Couples.* New York: Knopf, 1968.

Wachowiak, Dale, and Hannelore Bragg. "Open Marriage and Marital Adjustment." *Journal of Marriage & Family* 42.1 (1980): 57-72.

Waskul, Dennis. *Net.SeXXX: Readings on Sex, Pornography, and the Internet.* New York: Peter Lang, 2004.

Watson, J., & Watson, M. A. "Children of Open Marriages: Parental Disclosure and Perspectives." *Alternative Lifestyles* 5.1 (1982): 54-62. [Reported; not found.]

Weil, Bonnie Eaker. *Adultery: The Forgivable Sin.* Poughkeepsie: Hudson House, 2003.

Weitzman, Geri. "Therapy with Clients Who Are Bisexual and Polyamorous." *Journal of Bisexuality* 6.1/2 (2006): 137-164.

Weitzman, Geri. "What Psychology Professionals Should Know About Polyamory," March 1999. 30 Mar. 2009 <http://www.polyamory .org/~joe/polypaper.htm>.

Whisman, Mark A., Kristina Coop Gordon, and Yael Chatav. "Predicting Sexual Infidelity in a Population-Based Sample of Married Individuals." *Journal of Family Psychology.* 21.2 (2007): 320-324.

Whisman, Mark A., and Douglas K. Snyder. "Sexual Infidelity in a National Survey of American Women: Differences in Prevalence and Correlation as a Function of Method of Assessment." *Journal of Family Psychology* 21.2 (2007): 147-154.

www.ingramcontent.com/pod-product-compliance
Lightning Source LLC
Chambersburg PA
CBHW071218050326
40689CB00011B/2359